WATCH OUT
for the
HALLWAY

Our Two-Year Investigation

of the Most Haunted Library

in North Carolina

WATCH OUT
for the
HALLWAY

Our Two-Year Investigation
of the Most Haunted Library
in North Carolina

TONYA & JOEY MADIA

Visionary Living Publishing/Visionary Living, Inc.
New Milford, Connecticut

Watch Out for the Hallway:
Our Two-Year Investigation of the Most Haunted Library in North Carolina

Copyright Tonya and Joey Madia, 2018

Front and back cover by Chuck Regan
Interior and back cover design by Leslie McAllister

ISBN: 978-1-942157-39-7 (pbk.)
ISBN: 978-1-942157-40-3 (ebook)

Visionary Living Publishing/Visionary Living, Inc.
New Milford, Connecticut
www.visionarylivingpublishing.com

DEDICATION

This book is dedicated to Joey's Aunt Annette and Tonya's Grandma Donath. They were our spiritual teachers in life and continue to be in death.

ACKNOWLEDGMENTS

Our sincere thanks go to:

Steve Ward and Emily Mittermaier for reading an early draft of the manuscript and providing invaluable feedback and enthusiasm.

Our two mediums in training, Jolie Madia and Bryon Bartlett. Your willingness to share your gifts and commitment to the art of mediumship elevated each and every investigation of which you were a part.

Jonathan Edwards and the staff at Port City Tour Company for giving us the opportunity to spend 70-plus nights investigating the most haunted library in North Carolina.

The hundreds of guest investigators, including sensitives and mediums, who joined us the past two years.

The Mothman Irregulars—you taught us how to be good investigators and are the best friends anyone could ask for.

And, most importantly, to Dr. Thompson, John, Jerry, Michael, and all the many spirits who were gracious and patient enough to share their stories and ongoing experiences at the Webb with us.

TABLE OF CONTENTS

FOREWORD
Steve Ward

Have you ever gone back and looked at the chain of events that allowed you to be in just the right place and at the right time to have met some of your really good friends? When I thought about it I realized that my connection to Joey and Tonya started with swamp gas.

Yes, swamp gas. Allow me to explain. When I was in junior high there was a wave of UFO sightings and landings in Michigan in March of 1966, virtually in my backyard. Some claimed that it was just swamp gas, but for me the invading alien hordes had arrived. My fascination with all things unexplained had begun. In November of that same year, something even more exciting occurred. Two couples were chased by a winged humanoid creature in their automobile in Point Pleasant, West Virginia and the legend of the Mothman was born. I would, in a sense, be following the mystery of the Mothman for the rest of my life and would take many trips into the Ohio Valley as I was drawn by the many strange events that occurred there, such as UFO sightings and other paranormal phenomena. There I met two brothers, John and Tim Frick, who not only were an integral part of the annual Mothman Festival and fellow paranormal researchers but also were at the center of a truly awesome circle of friends.

Enter Joey and Tonya Madia who were part of that circle. In the Prologue you will see how Joey and Tonya first came to Point Pleasant, but if it hadn't been for swamp gas, Mothman, and the Frick brothers, we never would have crossed paths, and that would have been a shame.

When I first met the Madias on one of their visits to Point Pleasant, I discovered two fascinating and completely unassuming people. Not only were they just fun to be with, they had also experienced the paranormal in their lives separately and together. They even lived in a haunted "holler" for a time where "high strangeness" events were often present: ghosts, shadowy figures, and fairy lights were common.

I was, however, completely unprepared for just how talented and accomplished they were. Tonya, for example, is a Reiki Master, a yoga teacher, and a massage therapist. She is also a gifted medium—a talent she has put to good use for her investigations at the Webb Library. Last year she published her first book, *Living the Intuitive Life.* Joey is an author, playwright, actor, director, and book and music reviewer (to name only a few accomplishments) and has mentored and inspired thousands of students in workshops involved in theater and creative writing. (Gasp!) I have often wondered how I would have viewed the Madias during our first encounter if I had known all these things up front. Of course, any intimidation I might have felt would have been short-lived because, in fact, they are the most accessible and down to earth people I know.

While I have always been in awe of their accomplishments, envy has never entered in, but that may have recently changed. The reason is that these two individuals have stumbled onto a virtual laboratory in which they have been able to investigate continuing paranormal activity on a weekly basis for a period of two years. It was an amazing find that most researchers in the field would have given anything to uncover. This "laboratory" is the Webb Memorial Library in Morehead City, North Carolina, and for whatever reason it is an absolute hotbed of unexplained phenomena: mischievous spirits, ghostly apparitions, classic haunting phenomena, as well as the type of ghost that will take the time to have conversations with you. Images of people have been captured on film. Where there were no people—at least living ones. Believe it or not, there even seems to be a possible UFO connection to some of the events in and around the library.

Not only are we fortunate that this great resource has been uncovered, but we can be equally grateful that Joey and Tonya have been the lead investigators of this mysterious edifice. They led many tours and groups of people in the library, allowing them to experience the different manifestations for themselves. The Madias have used tools of the trade such as a device (a sort of a modified radio) called a spirit box, through which anomalous voices can be broadcast and recorded, and may represent the voices of those who have passed on. Tonya, using her mediumistic abilities, provided a balance to a strictly nuts and bolts approach. The blending of the two different techniques is part of the investigative style that Joey and Tonya have developed over time to collect information and seek out answers. During the tours the guests were always encouraged to use their talents as well, both mediumistic and observational. The result has provided a wealth of information from different sources meticulously chronicled and cataloged by the authors, which resulted in this amazing book.

I have been with Joey and Tonya in the dead of night in haunted areas like the lair of the Mothman outside of Point Pleasant while high strangeness was afoot. I watched them—even as they were experiencing the unknown—keep a cool head, balance skepticism with a sense of wonder and afterwards analyze objectively what had happened to them. They have applied the same approach to their research into the mysteries of the Webb Library. As you read this chronicle of the strange and travel to the different floors and areas in the library, you will meet an amazing cast of characters. A few will be among the living; however, most of them will be deceased. You will feel as if you are part of the investigative team looking into shadows, listening for that faint whisper and perhaps you will find yourself turning around and looking behind you, just in case. Join the Madias and their daughter, Jolie (a medium in her own right), as they embark on their great adventure.

.

PROLOGUE
Did You See That
An Unexpected Interdimensional

"I have amazing news!"

Tonya sounded unusually excited.

"What is it?" Joey asked. Had we come into some money? Did she get a promotion? Was grass finally growing on our rocky three acres in a West Virginia hollow?

"The Mothman Museum is only three hours away, right on the Ohio border! Wanna go?"

"Not really, babe. No."

For a writer, Joey had never been particularly adventurous.

Several years earlier, we saw *The Mothman Prophecies*, the 2002 film with Richard Gere and Laura Linney about the sightings of a winged creature in Point Pleasant in the 1960s, which culminated in the death of 46 people when the Silver Bridge collapsed.

Although we liked the film for its paranormal horror aspects, artistic direction by Mark Pellington, and its ambient-techno soundtrack, Joey had no intention of driving almost three hours to the Ohio border to visit a museum about a weirdly named supernatural being.

But Tonya persisted, appealing to Joey's desire for a weekend getaway and break from everyday life. Two years later, he finally agreed. Wanting some context in order to separate the fiction of the film from the facts, we ordered Jeff Wamsley's excellent books on the Mothman phenomenon. We also read John Keel's book, *The Mothman Prophecies,* on which the movie was based and derived its name, before we made the trip.

Having made arrangements for the kids, we booked a couple of weekend nights at the historic Lowe Hotel, which was rumored to be haunted. If we were driving all that way, we might as well stay in style and maybe see a ghost.

On August 21, 2009 we crossed the Ohio River on Route 2 into Point Pleasant, and we instantly knew we had made an excellent choice.

Point Pleasant is a sleepy little town stuck in time. Its quaint, quiet Main Street of restaurants and shops invites relaxation. It harkens back to a simpler time of strong, working-class values, family, and humility. It also sits at the confluence of two rivers, the Ohio and Little Kanawha, which may account for why it is so filled with paranormal activity.

We pulled up to the Lowe and were immediately taken with its architecture and energy. The owners, Ruth and Rush, were friendly and accommodating. While they were checking us in, Joey admired the photo of Will Patton, who was a standout performer in the *Mothman Prophecies*, hanging by the desk, while Tonya admired the spacious lobby adorned with antiques and marble pillars. The furnishings and oriental rugs made the Lowe feel homey and nostalgic.

After a little rest, we set out for some food. We decided on the Harris Steakhouse, also known as the Mothman Diner. Just like at the Lowe, the owner, Carolin Harris, and her staff were friendly and welcoming. We were taken by the dozens of drawings of the Mothman taped to the walls and found it kind of funny that the Steakhouse, which couldn't have been more than 20 feet wide, was divided into sections marked Smoking and Non-Smoking. The original soda fountain counter and jukebox, like the fixtures of the Lowe, served to transport us decades back in time.

After a delicious home-cooked meal and some friendly conversation with some of the locals, we made our way to the Mothman Museum. It was great to see so many props, costumes, and pictures from the film, and to learn a bit more about the legend of the Mothman and the tragedy of the Silver Bridge from their poster-sized newspaper reproductions, scale models, and videos.

We did the touristy thing of buying t-shirts and postcards for us and the kids and asked the guys behind the counter what else there was to do.

"You should visit the igloos," one of them suggested.

Igloos in West Virginia, Joey thought. *Man, this town is weird.*

The museum attendants explained that the igloos were made of concrete, not ice, and were used to store TNT manufactured at a local plant during World War II. The igloos were covered with earth and grass to camouflage them in case of enemy flyovers.

It sounded interesting enough to take the 20-minute drive to see them in what is now the McClintock Wildlife Management Area.

As we headed out the door, map in hand, Joey spotted a shop called The Point, which looked like another good place to buy some souvenirs. Wandering the aisles full of Native American and, of course, Mothman-themed merchandise, we said hello to the man behind the counter, who had hair like Elvis, a voice like Johnny Cash, and a pack of Marlboros rolled up in his sleeve.

He said his name was Bob and we got to talking. When we mentioned we were heading out to McClintock, known locally as the "TNT area" or just "the TNT," he asked to see our map. He made a few additional marks and gave us a little more background. He also mentioned that it was a former Indian burial ground. Now he had our full attention. We both had been studying Native American rituals and practices since 2002.

Bob also showed us some intriguing photographs of orbs and various anomalies he and other visitors had taken in the TNT—especially in the igloos—and asked that we please share with him any anomalous photos we might get. Because of our training in Native American rituals and shamanism, we purchased a bundle of sage to leave as an offering and went on our way.

The drive out to the igloos on Route 62 was pleasant and uneventful. It was a gorgeous day, not too hot, with a sky so blue it looked like one from a jigsaw puzzle. Following the markings on the map, we parked the car and crossed the graffiti-filled guardrail that led to the place where three open igloos reportedly were.

When we crossed the threshold and entered the woods, things got a little odd. Given the beauty of both the day and the scenery, the area just before the igloos should have evoked feelings of peace and calm as we looked at the birds and the trees. (Joey described it as looking like an image from a Ducks Unlimited pamphlet.) We both felt unsettled, like someone was watching us. The energy of the place also seemed disturbed. Even dark. We ventured into the first igloo and shot some pictures with a digital camera. At the second igloo, Joey felt a sour energy, as if a wall of negative energy blocked the entrance. He could not get any closer than a few feet or so from the doorway. He managed to snap some photos from the outside before having to beat a hasty retreat before he lost his lunch. (A fellow investigator who read an early proof of this book reported that she also "could not move past the threshold of igloo #2" in 2009.)

The third igloo was only about 20 feet farther away. As we started up the path, Joey's nausea got worse and we decided not to get any closer to it. Joey was trying his best not to be sick. The feeling of being watched was stronger than before.

We were in the TNT area for all of 15 minutes before we put the sage beneath some brush between the first and second igloos and got into the car to go back to town.

As we were returning to Point Pleasant on Route 62, talking about the irony of such dark sensations on such a beautiful day, we both saw a black shadow-like entity, perhaps a few hundred feet in front of us, launch itself across the road and disappear at the threshold of a cornfield. Not *into* the cornfield. It just blinked out *at the edge of it*.

If we both had not said, at the same instant, "Did you see that?" we would have independently dismissed it as a trick of the light or some other easily explainable event, and not even mentioned it to one another. There were cars in front of us and you'd think their drivers would have been slamming on the brakes if something had jumped in front of them. We decided not to describe the details to each other until later. At dinner that evening, we each drew what we saw. The pictures are virtually identical in their framing and contents.

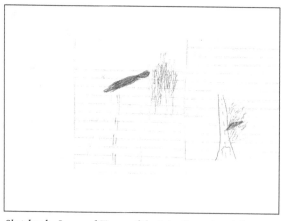

Sketches by Joey and Tonya of the interdimensional they saw.

xviii

As you can see from the drawings, it was a blob-like entity with a vague human shape, but with no discernible details. Joey has always described it as "a man in a jet-black neoprene wetsuit having just been fired from a cannon." Tonya has always described it as looking like a man but moving like a deer.

When we arrived in town, we decided to go back to The Point to tell Bob about our experience. We were surprised to find it was closed. Glancing at a cell phone, we discovered we could not account for 45 minutes of missing time!

Seeing movement inside the shop, we knocked on the door. Bob came out of the back room and unlocked it. After we told him what we saw, he gave us the card of two brothers who were longtime investigators of the Mothman and UFO/Men in Black phenomena in Point Pleasant. He said that they would be interested in hearing about what we'd seen.

We left them a message the next day and quickly forgot we did so, going about our daily lives as busy parents and career people.

A few months later, we received a call from one of the two brothers, John Frick, and set up a weekend to meet in Point Pleasant in November of that year.

Those two weekends in August and November of 2009 forever changed the trajectory of our lives. Our experience was interesting enough to John that he contacted a few other paranormal investigators, and they joined us in recreating our journey and in examining the area where we saw the shadow-like entity blink in and out of our reality.

There are a few things that are interesting about what we discovered during that first investigation—and there were several more in the years to come. First, Joey was sure that just before the place where we saw the shadow-like entity appear there was a gas station with colorful triangular flags strung between the light poles in the parking lot, but when we drove down Route 62 with the group of investigators there was no gas station. Furthermore, we never found any evidence of one ever being in that location.

Also, we both were sure there were cornfields on both sides of the road. But that was impossible, as there was a house on the left side as you drive back into town. Another aspect tied to these two anomalies, which we realized as we drove back into town after the investigation, was that our sense of distance and where landmarks were in relation was way off. The drive back on the day we saw the shadow-like entity seemed much longer than we now realized it was. There was an interesting copse of trees next to the house opposite the cornfield that produced some interesting electromagnetic frequency (EMF) readings, leading one of the investigators to postulate that it might be a portal. Portals were fairly unfamiliar to us at the time (so we thought) but thanks to our experiences in the Webb we now are intimately familiar with them—and had been for many years prior without understanding what they are. More on that later. In a line with where the shadow-like entity blinked out just before the cornfield is the American Electric Power plant. Perhaps that power plant contributes to the existence of the portal. If this is the case, what we saw was almost certainly an interdimensional that passed from another plane of existence into ours and back out again.

There is also the mystery of the missing 45 minutes and the phantom gas station and second cornfield. Considering them together, we surmise that time compressed and space stretched at the instant the portal opened and we saw the interdimensional.

Subsequently, we have visited Point Pleasant over a dozen times to investigate the activity still going on there. During those visits we had other odd experiences, which we detail in the next chapter.

Although we had encountered ghosts and other entities prior to our visit to Point Pleasant, what we saw and experienced that August day eight and a half years ago opened us up to a whole new range of phenomena, some of which, as you will read about in this book, affected what happened to us in the Webb.

1
If You Are So Powerful, Do Something to Us
Our Experiences with the Paranormal
Prior to the Webb

Tonya's Experiences

I was five years old the first time I remember having a paranormal experience. I was playing Barbies in my bedroom when I heard a faint voice calling my name. It sounded as if the voice came from either the hallway, or from my parents' bedroom across the hall. I thought my mother was calling me, and I set my Barbie down and went in search of her. I didn't find her in the hallway, so I went into her bedroom. She was not there. I walked to the end of the hallway to the bathroom, thinking she must be in that room. The bathroom was also empty, so I checked my brother's bedroom and found no one there either.

I decided I must have been hearing things and returned to my bedroom to continue playing with my dolls. As I sat down to play and reached for my Barbie I made an unnerving discovery: her head was missing! Baffled, I looked around my room for it. As I searched, I again heard my name being called. This time, it sounded as if the voice came from downstairs, and once again I thought my mother was calling me. I left my room and went downstairs to find her.

When I asked my mother what she wanted, she said she hadn't called me. Confused, I returned to my room to resume the search for my Barbie's missing head. What I found instead was even more unsettling; the entire Barbie was gone! I searched every inch of my room without success. At a loss to explain the disappearance, I went downstairs to tell my mother what had happened. She dismissed the incident offhand, suggesting I had either forgotten where I'd placed the doll, or that my brother was playing a joke on me. My brother was watching television in the living room and had been nowhere near my room, and I knew that I hadn't misplaced her. Frustrated, I returned to my room. There on the floor, exactly where I had left her when I heard my name the first time, was my Barbie, her head back on her neck. I went downstairs to join my brother in front of the television and would not return to my room for the rest of the day.

Strange events such as this occurred throughout my childhood. I was always hearing things. I would awaken in the middle of the night and hear voices, as if people were having a conversation, coming from downstairs. Thinking my parents were up, I would wander down to see them, only to find no one. I frequently heard footsteps wandering the upstairs hallway at night. Occasionally, I heard those footsteps make their way into my bedroom and I sank beneath my covers in fear.

Toys and cherished items frequently vanished. Sometimes they turned up days or weeks later; sometimes they were never seen again. I often felt as if I was being watched, and on occasion I was sure I felt someone stroking my hair. I remember always assuming ghosts were the cause of these unexplained events, even though I can't remember how, at such an early age, I had any idea about ghosts. It's almost as if I was born with the knowledge that they existed.

My paternal grandmother, Clara, was a medium, so it may be that conversations about the supernatural filtered into my subconscious from the time I was a baby. Grandma Clara visited frequently and she always brought her Ouija board with her. The Ouija was almost like an addiction for my grandmother; she couldn't get enough of it. My parents indulged her and participated in Ouija sessions with her whenever she

2

came to visit. Although I wasn't allowed to participate until I was older, I remember watching with astonishment as the planchette moved across the board, spelling out messages. The messages were always carefully transcribed into spiral bound notebooks. When my grandmother passed I became the custodian of the large cardboard box containing those notebooks, and I hope to compile many of the most intriguing transcripts into a book all its own.

Grandma Clara spent most of her adult life studying spiritualism, mediumship, and the supernatural. I was fortunate that she shared much of what she knew about dreamwork, meditation, astral travel, automatic writing, and telepathy with me. I readily absorbed all that she taught me; however, it was not until I was an adult that I put what I'd learned to use. Unexplained occurrences continued to follow me throughout my childhood and into adulthood.

One such experience occurred in 1991. I was living in Mesa, Arizona, and a friend of mine invited me to join her for a day trip to the historic town of Tucson. The drive from Mesa to Tucson was about two hours, and near the halfway point we were hungry. We hadn't seen anything for miles, so we were surprised when we came across a small diner sitting beside this lonely stretch of highway. Entering the diner was like taking a 40-year step back in time. The interior and all the fixtures looked as if they were straight from the 1950s, as did the man behind the register near the front door. He motioned for us to sit anywhere, and we crossed the room and slid onto red vinyl bench seats on either side of a Formica table. There was only one other occupied table in the place, so we were confused when, after almost 10 minutes, the waitress appeared at our table, exasperated. She apologized for the delay, explaining it was due to the "lunch rush" they were experiencing. My friend and I scanned the near-empty diner and returned our attention to the waitress in her light blue dress and white apron, poised to take our order. I hadn't seen a waitress uniform like that for many years. After the waitress hurried off with our orders, I commented to my friend that I was pretty sure Elvis was in the kitchen preparing the food. When the check came we were amazed at the total, which again was consistent with a 40-year time gap.

I often joke that when we arrived in Tucson it was closed. That isn't *exactly* true, but we hadn't planned our trip well and many of the attractions we planned to see were closed because it was Sunday. We were disappointed and walked around for about an hour before heading back to Mesa. On the way home we decided to stop at the diner for a snack. There was little on that lonely stretch of highway, so the small diner should have been easy to locate. We watched for a good part of the trip and never found it. It was as if it had been nothing more than a mirage in the middle of the desert.

Years later I learned that occurrences like my diner experience are reported all over the world and are frequently referred to as "time slips."

My strange experiences never seemed to end, and most of the homes I've lived in were riddled with unexplained activity.

One such home was a house in Mesa that I moved into with my two sons in 1996. I began having nightmares the first night we spent there. My oldest son, Daniel, complained of an uneasy feeling and the sense that he was being watched. My son Jeremy, who was only two, frequently pointed at what appeared to be nothing on the staircase while saying "scary." On one occasion I found Jeremy lying face down on the floor, unable to move, as if someone was holding him down.

The final straw came a few weeks later. As I was applying makeup in the upstairs bathroom I heard a sinister witch-like cackle so close to me that I felt the cold breath of the being in my ear. I moved us out of that house as soon as I could. It didn't solve the problem—I continued to be plagued by the strange for many years to come.

I was 40 years old when I finally decided I was ready to face my fear of the unknown and get to the bottom of these experiences. I became interested in investigating locations known for paranormal activity and was excited to learn that one such location, Point Pleasant, West Virginia, was only a few hours away.

Joey's Experiences

When it first became certain that we were going to write this book, and the opening chapter consisted of us talking about our experiences with the paranormal, I was a little concerned. Tonya's gifts as a medium and healer are immense and impressive. I did not have much in the way of psychic abilities, although the nearly two years we spent investigating the Webb Memorial Library enhanced my ability to hear spirits and interdimensionals through clairaudience. One night in October 2017 I correctly predicted that the four guest investigators joining us at the

Webb would be a couple in their 50s and two young women. By February 2018 I was seeing the head-and-shoulder outlines of spirits as they moved around in both our home and the Webb.

My engagement with the paranormal began when I was a junior in high school. Before that time, I have no memories of anything from beyond the veil intruding on my life in any way. In the years before high school I lived in a small town on the "other side of the tracks" and spent many days—and nights—playing in the woods in old, abandoned houses and burned out buildings, and I don't recall a single time my hackles went up. I had my friends—a capable band of stick-gun, aluminum-garbage-can-cover shield warriors on banana-seat bikes (*Stand by Me* meets *Stranger Things*)—and, as youth often are, we were fearless.

But not when it came to horror films. At least I wasn't. More like Major Coward. I did like the opening of the Chiller features, with the hand coming out of the ground and the monster-like voice speaking that word, "Chillllllllerrrrrrr" that I watched with my brother and father. But Freddie Krueger? Jason? *The Exorcist*? No thanks. I always took a pass.

In my sophomore year of high school, I had an experience that convinced me that what people called "the paranormal" was real. Two girls in the theater club started playing with a Ouija board. I was familiar with them—my aunt and uncle had one in a stack of games in the attic room where the kids hung out on holidays and we would set it up and spell things out (probably dirty words and other silly things). We had no idea what a Ouija board was.

Back to my sophomore year. A few of us would gather after school in the drama room and the girls let us sit in on their sessions. It started innocently enough, as Ouija board experiences often do. They met a little girl from "Colonial Times" and she liked to play with them, to make them laugh. This went on for a couple of afternoons. She then told the two girls she had been murdered—strangled and dumped in a river—and that the man who murdered her was still pursuing her. Of course, the two girls became concerned and more emotionally involved, which is what the low-vibrational spirits who come through the Ouija board want. Especially when the little girl became increasingly more frightened and no longer wanted to talk. She grew more distant until, one afternoon, the spirit of the killer revealed his true identity. He told my two friends that he had been *pretending* to be the little girl all along.

By this time, like word of a schoolyard brawl, news of the Ouija sessions had made it through the grapevine (no Internet or smartphones then—just good old word of mouth) and our group grew to about 10, most of whom wanted to stop the sessions all together when the murderer made his reveal.

The two girls began meeting in the basement of one of their houses after school, continuing to use the board to contact different spirits, most of which were as nasty as the murderer. One day, emotionally drained from their experiences, they didn't come to school.

A close friend of mine decided something should be done, and I readily agreed. We went over to the house where the Ouija board was set up in the basement. There were candles lit throughout the room and about a dozen other kids who had heard what we were up to were gathered to witness whatever was going to happen.

The two girls put their hands on the planchette and started to get communications from the murderer. A low-level hysteria worked its way through the room. My friend and I challenged the murderer:

"Leave the girls alone!" we commanded. "If you are so powerful, do something to us! Make something happen to us!"

Youth.

The girls begged us to stop, but we kept on provoking it. The planchette moved faster. We provoked the murderer further, "Come on! Do something! Do something to us!"

The candles all went out. And I swear, for an instant, all sound dissolved and my heart ceased to beat. It was like all light and life were sucked out of the room.

That was the end of the Ouija board. It would be many years before I put my hands on a planchette. And only with two well-trained mediums in the room to guide the session.

From that time on, I believed there were things beyond the veil that could harm us. That existed outside the realms of accepted science. And I didn't care to know much about them. I adopted a "live and let live" philosophy after my near-escape from that basement in New Jersey in 1985 that lasted 15 years.

Then I met Tonya. And, as she always quotes me as saying before an investigation at the Webb, "The spirits were investigating us, so we started investigating back." And that is really the truth of it. I can only take so much mystery, and I've never been a fan of surprises.

My journey beyond paranormal detecting equipment into genuine, first-hand experiences of the paranormal has come through my studies of shamanism and lucid dreaming. These studies triggered astral travel and, according to various Reiki masters and shamans, I bring a lot of energetic "junk" back with me from my travels, which has to be cleared from my etheric body every so often by energy healers.

As a longtime professional writer, many of my stories deal with the paranormal, and my dreams—lucid and otherwise—and astral travels have offered me a rich array of experiences and new acquaintances from beyond the veil. As the decades have progressed, I have realized that I *have to* write about these experiences, because some are so absolutely frightening I have to manage them through the act of writing or they might damage my psyche. I have been taken into caves and temples on more than one occasion where I was cut into pieces (an aspect of shamanic initiation in many cultures) or set on fire or put through some other strange ritual. If I didn't wake up or otherwise come out of the trance I was in, I know that, on a cellular level, I would have been forever changed to the point that the "normal life" of a father and husband would no longer be possible. As I get older and my abilities more attuned, I spend more and more time in parallel universes while I sleep, where I have a whole different set of projects that I work on while I'm there. Sometimes it takes several minutes while I awaken to discern what belongs in which universe.

In the rest of this chapter, you will read about the many paranormal experiences we have shared during our 20 years together.

As long as the spirits of former human beings and other entities keep investigating us, we'll keep on being curious about them and seeking better, more well-rounded ways to learn at least some of the mysteries of what's behind the veil.

Our Experiences Together

In our travels over the past 20 years, we have lived in and visited several places filled with unexplained events. Although no one can say for sure exactly why a place is haunted, there are several theories, and they have helped us to not only make sense of some of the experiences we had in the Webb but also in other locations where the paranormal has investigated us.

We have experienced "haunting" activity in every house we have lived in. It took years for us to understand that the whole world is "haunted." What we often refer to as "paranormal" activity is a normal condition of our planet, albeit beyond the tools of current science and technology to fully understand. The difference for us is that we notice it.

And that noticing creates a feedback loop that, along with Tonya's developed abilities and those of our teenage daughter, Jolie, makes the chances of our engaging with the paranormal no matter where we live or visit almost a certainty.

Our first several years together, when we met and married in Mesa, Arizona, were a fairly tumultuous time as we learned to live together and Joey adjusted to being a father to two young boys. We were so involved in the challenges of those early years that we didn't notice much else around us. Our mutual experiences with the paranormal began in an apartment in New Jersey in 2000. During our years at this apartment, we experienced strange, and sometimes humorous, occurrences. Finding humor in the unknown when you can is essential when appropriate. It helps diminish the fear that comes with facing things we don't fully understand.

We termed one such occurrence "the stinky old man" because of the nature of the phenomenon. We would be sitting in the living room when, out of nowhere, a strange odor manifested right next to us. The odor was distinctly that of a person who was in desperate need of a shower. It lingered from a few minutes to a few hours and then vanished as quickly as it manifested. The odor also moved around the room, as if whatever it was attached to was moving around the room. Try as we might, we were never able to fully identify the cause of this terrible smell. Fortunately, the phenomenon did not follow us when we moved out of the apartment. Jolie, who was a toddler at the time, often pointed and asked who was walking down the hallway, when she and Tonya were the only ones at home.

One night while Tonya was doing the dishes, Jolie entered the kitchen from the living room and told her there was an old man on the couch. Tonya ran into the living room and found the couch—and the room—empty. Another time while Tonya was alone in the apartment washing dishes she felt something lightly tap her heels. She looked down to see Jolie's bouncy ball, which had been sitting quite still in front of the sofa the last she had seen it. For the ball to reach Tonya's feet, it would have to roll several feet and turn two sharp corners.

One of the most frightening experiences that we had took place between 2004 and 2005. After months of searching, we signed a one-year lease on a three-bedroom Cape Cod in Tinton Falls, New Jersey. Activity began from the moment we moved in and continued for the 11 months that we lived there.

Like Act I of most haunted house stories, our hopes for this particular place were high. We were about to open a school for the performing arts with a trusted friend of Joey's, with whom he'd been working since high school. In order to control costs and have the convenience of being able to meet and plan whenever we wanted, we decided that he would move in with us. The kids were thrilled. He was like a godfather to them. So much so, they called him uncle. The kids were also excited because, for the first time, they would each have their own room and a large yard in which to play. We were all excited. Unfortunately, it wasn't long before our excitement turned to fear. In fact, from the first day it seemed as if our time in that house would be overshadowed by bad experiences. They started as minor inconveniences, mostly mundane, but it didn't take long for things to ramp up.

On the day we moved in, we learned that the master bedroom, located in the finished basement, was flooded. About a week after the work was complete and we were finally settling in, we noticed a fine black film covering everything in the basement. We had no idea what it was. We wiped it off only to find it again the next day. After a few days of this, the heating system suddenly stopped working. By now it was well into December. We called a heating and cooling repairman (chosen randomly—so we thought—from the phone book) to come and take a look.

Tonya will never forget the look on the repairman's face when she opened the door upon his arrival. The kids were at school and Joey and our business partner were off on separate appointments. She thought it odd and more than a bit unsettling the way the repairman seemed to glare at her as she said hello and thanked him for coming. His expression was so penetrating, in fact, that as she led him downstairs to the furnace she wondered if he was going to be ill-mannered and difficult to deal with.

As they descended the staircase, he asked her questions about things he couldn't have possibly known about. He asked about her grandmother Clara—by name—and told Tonya that she was with her all the time. He asked who in the house was writing about knights and dragons, a reference to Joey's first novel, which would not be published for another four years, and went on to describe Joey, whom he'd never met, in unsettling detail. Tonya often thinks about how silly she must have looked as she stood there, mouth open in amazement, while he went into more detail about her grandmother and relayed messages from her about conversations that had taken place between her and Tonya years before her death.

The repairman (whom we refer to when relating this story as Jack, in the interest of privacy and as an homage to both F. Paul Wilson's anti-hero and Steve Ward, a close friend and talented paranormal investigator who first recommended Wilson's books to us) went on to explain that he was a medium and that he could see that, like Grandma Clara, Tonya also had "the gift." Jack assured her that with training and guidance she could become as proficient at "seeing" as he was and offered to come by the house on evenings and weekends to share his knowledge and experience. After inspecting the furnace, he found nothing wrong with it except a missing filter; this was the reason for the black soot. (We had not checked the filter as we assumed it had been replaced as a matter of course prior to our moving in.) It turned out that Jack's discovery may have saved us from carbon monoxide poisoning. The heater malfunction was so curious that, looking back, we are confident that someone, perhaps Grandma Clara, was looking out for us.

Who better to send than a fellow medium who could clearly understand her messages?

As Jack was leaving, our business partner pulled into the driveway. Jack approached him and told him not to feel bad about something he had witnessed when he was just a boy. His guilt was unnecessary. There was nothing he could have done. Jack also cautioned him to watch his speed—he had a habit of driving too fast and it would get him into trouble.

When Jack returned a few weeks later, so much was going on in the house that Tonya was more interested in having him do a reading on the space than starting her lessons in mediumship. As she led him room to room through the house, she shared what we had been experiencing.

The phenomena began in our son Jeremy's room. Tonya explained that Jeremy had been complaining that every night around 3 AM he woke up to his stereo or ceiling fan turning on by itself. One early morning he woke up to witness two people, a man and a young woman, playing out an agitated scene on his television, *which was turned off.* The scene culminated in the man choking the young woman. Jeremy, who was 10 years old, was understandably shaken by this and left his room to sleep on the sofa.

Next, Tonya took Jack into Jolie's room. She was five and also was experiencing difficulty. Almost every night she awakened from terrible nightmares, something she had never complained of before. Tonya and Jack spent some time in the hallway, where Tonya shared that Jolie had twice witnessed a black mass floating toward the living room. They moved from the hallway into the living room, where Tonya shared with Jack how we often experienced a sense of unease accompanied by the feeling of being watched while in that room.

Tonya also explained to him what she and Joey were experiencing in our bedroom. Nearly every morning at 3 AM the telephone rang, yet there was never anybody on the line. When we answered, we often heard a series of clicks, beeps or static; sometimes there was only silence. Our bedroom, right at the foot of the stairs, did not have a door, so we used a bamboo curtain for privacy. There were a few times when the phone rang that we heard the curtain move.

Tonya told Jack how footsteps were often heard in conjunction with what sounded like a heavy ball bouncing across the floor in the third floor bedroom (our business partner's) when nobody was up there. Tonya also noted that on several occasions she had heard the voices of children coming from the basement when she was home alone.

What Tonya didn't share with Jack was the emotional changes we were all experiencing in the house. Because of being awakened at night, electronics going on, and nightmares, both Jeremy and Jolie were having a difficult time. But so were we adults.

It must be said that starting a new business, especially in the arts, is stressful. Plus, we were all learning to live together. Money was tight and the days and nights were long, but that does not account for the severity of the mood changes we underwent.

One afternoon, while planning out the curriculum for the theater program at the school, Joey and his longtime friend had a difference of opinion—about something fairly minor—that quickly escalated into a screaming match. Although they stood well apart in the kitchen, with the dining table that served as their workspace as a barrier between them, the vibe was one of pending violence. At the apex of the argument, Joey's friend stormed upstairs to his room. Joey heard several glass items breaking.

Our marriage was not faring much better. The problems with the house, the difficulties the kids were having, and the 3 AM calls were making a good night's sleep increasingly rare. We began getting on each other's nerves. One day, while Tonya was out on an appointment, Joey found her engagement, wedding, and five-year anniversary bands on her nightstand. Thinking in his agitation that it was a subtle message about her feelings, he took the rings and hid them in a porcelain theater mask that was hung on a long nail on the 4×4-inch oak beam that ran across their room.

When Tonya arrived home she immediately went to retrieve her rings, which she had innocently forgotten to put on after a shower. Joey was working at his computer on the far side of the room where the theater mask was facing. Tonya asked him if he had seen the rings. At first he played dumb, pressing her for why she hadn't been wearing them. They argued. As they did, the theater mask lifted off the nail (which stuck out at least an inch and a half). As the mask fell to the floor, the three rings flew out and landed on the bed, which was *behind* where the mask had been hanging.

One would be hard pressed to explain that happening using any traditional principles of physics.

Back to Jack's tour of the house. Before he and Tonya went back upstairs, she shared the encounters that both she and Joey were having in the house that, more than any of the other experiences, left us with the desire to move our family to a safer, more peaceful home.

The first encounter occurred one afternoon as Tonya stood in front of the bedroom mirror applying makeup. She noticed the reflection of a being standing behind her, its face peering just over her right shoulder. It was a humanoid figure dressed in a blue military jacket with fringed yellow epaulettes. The body and uniform stood in juxtaposition to the face, which was that of a pink hog with tusks. As soon as the figure appeared in the mirror, she shot around to look behind her and found nothing there. The encounter was so odd and happened so quickly that she dismissed it, not mentioning it to anyone.

Two days later the second encounter occurred. Tonya was in the kitchen preparing dinner when Joey arrived home and headed down to our bedroom. Before he reached the bottom of the stairs she heard him let out a startled yell, and he quickly scrambled back up the stairs to the kitchen. Joey explained that, as he neared the bottom of the stairs, he looked down to find a humanoid creature with a hog's head waiting for him just inside the bamboo curtain.

As Tonya poured coffee for her and Jack in the kitchen, he stated that what we were experiencing was poltergeist activity, most likely brought on by Jeremy's age, and that it would soon pass. He then hastily stated his need to be somewhere else, assuring Tonya that we had nothing to worry about and that he would be in touch to start her training.

She never heard from him again. She left a few messages for him, but her calls were not returned. Grandma Clara had taught Tonya enough about poltergeists to know that our experiences did not fit the criteria for what was happening. Poltergeist is German for "noisy ghost" and is a phenomenon that usually involves loud noises such as banging or knocking, and is frequently accompanied by objects moving about, often as if being thrown. The classic film by the same name begins with accurately portrayed poltergeist activity before devolving into a fantastical horror story. Our experiences in the house in Tinton Falls thankfully stopped short of a full-blown horror story, but there was still more to come.

As the activity increased, we spent more time on the weekends at Joey's parents' house. One of those weekends, Joey's business partner had gone to a wedding. He came home late in the evening and went into the bathroom. On the other side of the door he heard his cat pawing at the door and making sounds as though it were agitated. He went to see what was wrong and the bathroom door would not open. He tried for several minutes until, without explanation, it opened. By that time the cat had calmed down.

As things worsened, we got the sense that Joey's partner knew more about what was happening in the house than he was comfortable sharing. Not knowing where else to turn, we contacted Joey's aunt and uncle, who were well-trained spiritual healers and counselors. They agreed to come to the house.

After spending some time there, Joey's aunt, a to-the-point Italian-American Roman Catholic with an unwavering devotion to family, said, "Here's what I think. It's not just this house that's haunted—it's the entire block. Buy out your lease, take a financial loss, do whatever you have to—but get your family out of here."

Although we never discussed our experiences with our neighbors, they were involved in a renovation plagued by months of problems, from water leaks to structural issues, which put a strain on their finances and nerves.

Roughly a week later we were still uncertain what to do, when a decision was forced on us. At 3 AM a valve on the hot water heater burst, flooding the basement for a second time. Although there was nothing paranormal about an old hot water heater failing, this was the final straw. The time of night, 3 AM, could not be ignored—it was the "witching hour," when so much other phenomena occurred.

Immediately after moving all our belongings to a dry area of the basement, we agreed that Tonya and the kids would stay with Joey's parents until new living arrangements could be made. The landlord, embarrassed by the endless troubles with the house, let us out of our lease a month early without penalty.

We rented a small, overpriced townhouse that strained our bottom line, a situation we knew was only a temporary fix. Worn out by the financial and logistical challenges of living in New Jersey in the aftermath of 9/11, we decided it was time to give the kids a more relaxed pace of life. After looking at several potential states, a close friend offered us an opportunity to purchase three acres in the quiet West Virginia countryside. We sold our share of the theater school to our business partner and prepared for our new adventure.

Tucked into the hillside of a West Virginia hollow (or "holler," as the locals say, and we quickly adopted), our newly built home was designed to give us the serene lifestyle we envisioned. The move, however, was not without its challenges. There had been a month-long delay due to a dispute with the neighbors about where the electrical lines could be run, so we were staying with the friends who had bought acreage across the holler from us the previous year.

One afternoon, we decided to take a walk on the property between the two houses. We came across a swath of old barbed wire wrapped around a few trees. As we looked closer, we saw, tucked into the moss-covered trunk of one of the trees, what we can only describe as a miniature fairy village. Although no fairies were present, we could see the dwellings and features of the village. Joey suggested Tonya take a picture of it and, as she raised the camera, the idyllic vision faded away and we were left staring at only the barbed wire. We believe we witnessed something out of time and space. It would not be the last time a portal or other interdimensional doorway opened in that area. A few years later, Joey was looking out of our big living room window at that part of the landscape, which always held a strong pull and fascination for him and saw a bearlike creature walking on all fours along the roadway in front of the property. The vision just faded away, vanishing as it passed our house.

As we waited for the electricity to be run in our new house, all our belongings were stored in its basement, which, ironically, took on water during a bad rainstorm before the windows were properly sealed.

This resulted in weeks of drying out our belongings. Tonya had not yet started her new job and school had not started, so she took the kids to the house to work for several hours each day. Once the electric problem was settled, Joey suggested that she and the kids stay in the house while the final touches were completed.

Tonya was reluctant. Despite everything looking picture perfect, she found herself feeling uneasy in the house from the start, especially in the master bedroom. She had the overwhelming sense that she was being watched. As we settled in, odd things happened. Strange noises were a regular occurrence, particularly in Jolie's bedroom. Doors often closed by themselves. "Fairy lights" appeared in the house, starting small and growing in size before fading away. Objects, usually belonging to Joey, mysteriously disappeared and reappeared several hours or even days later. Tonya frequently awakened in the middle of the night to the sound of banging against the back of the house.

One night she woke to see the figure of a little girl standing next to our bed. Not long after, she decided to take photos on her cell phone when she felt the spirit was present. In one of the photos (lost when the phone died), what appears to be the face of a young girl is seen peeking through the closet door, which was slightly ajar when she took the photo. No one else was in the room when the photo was taken.

The little girl's story was related to Tonya through a dream during an afternoon nap. In the dream, a blonde pioneer girl of about

10 was hopelessly trying to find her way back to her homestead. After wandering for hours through the woods, she gave into exhaustion, and lay down next to a large tree, where she died. Tonya instantly recognized the tree as one of the oldest on our property.

Several months later Tonya was receiving a reading from a psychic who, without Tonya mentioning her, brought up the little girl, who he said was attached to Tonya, having become quite fond of her. He also pointed out that the girl thought Joey was much too serious (which was true) and she loved to play practical jokes on him by hiding items like his keys, to get him to lighten up a little.

Psychic and paranormal experiences through dreams became commonplace for Tonya during our years in "the holler," and many of the dreams focused on the area where we saw the fairy village and Joey saw the spectral bear. Paranormal investigator Rosemary Ellen Guiley later confirmed during a visit to our house what we had surmised all along—that the area, especially the space between two tall trees in the front of our property, was a portal.

Each of Tonya's dreams related to the portal area began the same way. Tonya would be staring out the window into the portal location. In one such dream, Tonya noticed a Cro-Magnon picking plants in that area. Moments later Jolie was in the yard with him and Tonya screamed for Jolie to come inside, away from the man. Unperturbed, Jolie took Cro-Magnon's hand and led him to the front porch where the man shape-shifted into a modern-looking senior with grey hair and glasses. The man introduced himself as George Washington, raising Tonya's suspicions. She pulled Jolie inside and closed the door.

Dreams within dreams were another common occurrence. A month after the Cro-Magnon dream, Tonya dreamt that she woke from a dream and sat up in her bed. She glanced toward the bedroom window and spotted a young boy, who appeared to be American Indian, peering into the bedroom. Tonya ran to the window and the boy ran to the portal area. Tonya opened the front door and called out to the boy, who made his way to the porch, at which point his head transformed into a giant mole. Tonya grabbed his snout and woke from the dream.

Another dream within a dream began with sleep paralysis. As she lay in bed, Tonya found herself unable to move. She heard knocking and thumping all around the house followed by someone whispering in her ear. She slipped into a dream in which she awoke and looked out the bedroom window. A picnic in a fairy circle had been prepared in the front yard. On her way to the front door she encountered little people who stood no more than several inches tall. Tonya told them how excited she was about the fairy circle; she leapt into the air and flipped back onto the bed. Once in the bed she fell back to sleep briefly, then sat up again.

When she again looked out the window, three American Indians were performing a ceremony in the circle. On her way to the front door she encountered a small, blue man with pointy ears. The man was grinning, and Tonya asked him his name. "Philolexi," he responded. Tonya invited him to sit and chat and he made his way to the sofa and climbed up. Just as he started to talk, Tonya awakened.

Our experiences with the portal in the "holler" gave us context and understanding when we began investigating the Webb, which has an area we call "the Portal Hallway" (see Chapter 12).

Activity continued in cycles for the seven years we lived in the "holler." Besides the little girl, other spirits made themselves known to us (one of which became quite fond of Jolie). The "fairy lights" and larger, orb-like lights the size of beach balls continued to appear to us and to our guests. We also had experiences with "little people" that we saw scurrying around our living room. One about a foot high also ran across our bed as we lay in it one afternoon.

By this time, we were years into our shamanic and Native American studies and had several friends from both the Shawnee and Lakota tribes. A Shawnee chief came to our house to visit and immediately noticed two things. One was that he pointed out the exact spot in the living room where the "little people" typically gathered. The second was that, a year before, out of nowhere, six sycamores began growing around our property where we had put a Lakota sweat lodge. Without a water source, the sycamores should not have been there. He told us they were there because of the sweat lodge. The Shawnee looked for sycamores for their settlements and holy sites because they knew water would be nearby. In this case, the Shawnee were acknowledging the holy site we had created.

This was interesting. When we first did Lakota rituals within the sweat lodge and on the property around it, we saw a steep increase in the paranormal activity within and around the house. Lakota sweat lodge rituals are powerful in and of themselves, and many unexplainable things happen in the darkness of the lodge as the songs are sung, steam made by pouring water on heated river rocks, pipes smoked, and spirits beseeched and welcomed through prayer. In addition to the expected phenomena, we could tell that the land and the spirits on it were in an agitated state.

One of our close friends with experience in Lakota ceremonies asked a simple question that unlocked the mystery, "Are you honoring all the tribal spirits who passed through this land, or just honoring the Lakota spirits, whose people never even settled here?"

We did some research right away because our answer was that we were honoring the Lakota spirits only. From the time we began naming all the tribes with ties to that geographic area, especially the Shawnee, the agitated energy went away.

By the time we sold the house to move on to our next adventure we were so accustomed to unusual occurrences that we were matter-of-fact about them. Our relaxed attitude about unusual phenomena was largely due to the research and investigations we were now undertaking due to our experience with the interdimensional we saw in Point Pleasant.

After that experience, detailed in the Prologue, our subsequent visits to Point Pleasant resulted in our encountering other strange phenomena in the TNT area, such as a dark, malevolent energy we encountered while investigating there a few years ago with a group that included the Frick brothers and others we met after our experience with the interdimensional. Joey and another investigator experienced nausea and extreme physical discomfort while encountering the energy, while Tonya and two other investigators noted an overwhelming sense of foreboding. The previous evening, two investigators had seen the energy manifest in the form of a large black shadow before feeling it pass right through them.

After another transitional year in an apartment after Jeremy graduated high school and went to New York City to pursue a career in the arts, we decided to try something completely new. In the summer of 2015 we moved to Beaufort, North Carolina, a quaint little town on the Crystal Coast in the southern Outer Banks, with a rich history of pirates and ghosts.

We lived there for nearly three years and experienced all manner of paranormal occurrences in the town and in our house, which was directly across from the former train station. One afternoon while doing the dishes, Joey looked out the window and saw a phantom train moving slowly down the street. We also had experiences at the Old Burial Ground, two blocks away, that dates to the early years of the 1700s. Some spirits followed us home or visited us from there. We also had several spirits that lived in the house with us—two of whom were males that spent a lot of time in Jolie's room. We also engaged with about half a dozen other spirits of a more transient nature that caused knocking, footsteps, flickering lights, jiggling door handles and other phenomena.

Our two-year investigation at the Webb Memorial Library certainly increased the activity in our home in Beaufort, although, as the experiences related in this chapter make clear, no matter where we are, the paranormal is eager to make itself known. Experiences we have had in other historic buildings, such as the Trans-Allegheny Lunatic Asylum in Weston, West Virginia and commercial buildings that we rented, worked in, and were invited to investigate in several states are numerous and detailed enough for a book all their own.

Through it all, we have learned a great deal about what approaches to investigating the paranormal work best—and what don't work at all, or work against the investigator in the field—and how our unique combination of skill sets and 20-year relationship combine to guide and structure our approach to this mysterious and challenging field.

In the next chapter, we detail our investigating style. We feel strongly that what makes our approach to investigating unique is our focus on story and context. Encounters with the paranormal are always exciting; however, what gives these experiences *meaning* is being able to identify—through research, interviews, anecdotal evidence, and the information the spirits provide—the stories that drive the phenomenon. We are excited to share these stories with you, and hope they go a long way to answering in the affirmative the age-old question: Does our consciousness survive death?

2
Your Own Bodies are the Best Equipment There Is
About Our Investigative Style

Think for a moment about your average paranormal show(s) on cable television—it doesn't matter which one specifically, because they are pretty much the same, and they can be easily split into two format types.

In the first (the ones we prefer), real people are interviewed about their experiences and there are cinematic reenactments intermixed. Perhaps one or two experts are also interviewed to enlighten the audience on the art and science of paranormal investigating. Some of these shows work well. If the interviewees are sincere and the actors and special effects people don't overdo it, much may be gleaned from these "case studies."

The second type of paranormal show is when a group of investigators—usually a male lead, a female who is a "medium" or a "sensitive" (for the purposes of this book, when we use the term "medium" we are talking about someone who can communicate with the dead, while a "sensitive" is someone who senses the energy of a spirit presence, and may even be able to hear or see them, but does not communicate with them) and one or more tech experts—go to a place that is known to be haunted. They will usually interview the owners or staff during the day and investigate at night, using a standard array of equipment: electromagnetic frequency (EMF) meters, temperature gauges, infrared cameras, night vision apparatus, and some form of "spirit box." These shows feel contrived. After all, what are the chances that the spirits will "perform" on command the way actors do? Because of Joey's involvement in the entertainment business and our knowing many paranormal investigators who have appeared on or hosted these shows, we know that much of what seems spontaneous is either rehearsed, or what you see is a later "take" to get the right angles, sound quality, and so on, and sometimes even fabricated or staged. This is understandable on a certain level—ratings would not be good if nothing or very little happened. Oftentimes experts and hosts struggle with the lack of integrity. That's show business, folks...

In many ways, our investigative style matches up with what you see in the types of shows we just mentioned. In this chapter we will outline our techniques, provide some larger context for why we think that education in a broad range of subjects is essential, and why, when it comes right down to it, as Tonya tells guest investigators before we start, "Your own bodies are the best equipment there is."

Our first visit to the Webb Memorial Library was on Sunday, May 22, 2016. A few weeks prior, Joey was getting ready to perform one of the historical education programs he has created for Port City Tour Company when he noticed an advertising poster on the wall of the shop:

"Haunted Webb Memorial, nightly paranormal investigations"

Given our background and experience, Joey was curious. The owner of Port City told him what the program had looked like in the past, adding that it wasn't currently running because the previous guides for the tour, who were not paranormal investigators per se, had left or were no longer interested. He was looking for someone to fill their spots.

Joey let the owner, Jonathan, know about our background and Tonya's psychic abilities. After his program, Joey went home to tell Tonya about it. It didn't take much conversation or contemplation on either side before we set up an "audition."

We prefer to know as little as possible about a place before we go in. The last thing we want is to get hooked into hearsay, assumptions, and wrong data that prevent us from being open-minded.

For reasons that the phenomena reported in this book will make clear, we were immediately impressed by the Webb. That first evening turned out to be informative and eventful; we encountered several spirits and even made a new friend—all of which we will discuss in detail in the chapters to come.

Tonya is most interested in her own psychic impressions as a starting point, so as we entered the building she allowed herself to be pulled into various areas and share with Joey and Jonathan what she was picking up. We had agreed ahead of time that Jonathan would not confirm or deny anything until we had gone through the entire building, which consists of two floors and a basement.

After exploring the building to get psychic impressions, we made our way back to some of the rooms where Tonya had picked up a lot of activity to try out the newly acquired, state of the art, P-SB11 device, or the "spirit box" as it is commonly known. We will use these two names interchangeably throughout the book. After considerable Internet research, it is unclear what the "P" stands for (paranormal? professional?). The "11" refers to this model being the eleventh design by the manufacturer. Used by many paranormal researchers as a way to communicate with the dead, the P-SB11 sweeps radio frequencies and provides white noise as a means for spirits to communicate via words, which are heard through the speakers. Joey describes how the box works with a metaphor: "It's like the sheen of steam on a mirror after a hot shower that allows you to write on it."

Although the spirit box as we now know it was only invented in 2002 by Frank Sumption—for years it was known as a "Frank's Box"—everyone from inventor Thomas Edison to poet and playwright William Butler Yeats experimented with and championed some form of machine to talk to the dead. The P-SB11 is a big improvement over the commercial and homemade spirit boxes of the past, many of which we have used. When the antenna is down and the radio function is turned off, the amount of radio chatter that comes through is drastically reduced. We can't tell you the hours we've spent at some diner at one in the morning arguing over the difference between a radio commentator and a communication from a spirit. We were quite pleased with our first experience using the P-SB11 and received several clear communications.

We went back to the Webb a few nights later, again with Jonathan, who had been impressed with what Tonya had picked up, much of which had come up in the past from previous investigators and their guests. There were new pieces of data as well.

At the end of the second night, we were officially the new team for the Haunted Webb Memorial paranormal investigations.

At this point, knowing we had only a few weeks before we would begin leading investigations, we talked to a few of the previous tour guides and some locals. Whenever possible, we talk to owners, staff, neighbors, and those who have lived or worked in the area for a while. This gives us a feel for how the haunted building or home fits into the fabric of the community and what the prevailing stories and legends are.

Once we have a good handle on the broad strokes of a site's history, we visit historical societies, courthouses, and other repositories of documents, newspapers, and photos that can provide the facts and figures about the site we are going to investigate. In the case of the Webb Memorial Library, this research was important, because there was a good deal of folklore and hearsay concerning the Wade House that stood on the site prior to the Webb being built. There was an elaborate story about the "Wade sisters," one of whom was young and pretty and the other a spinster, which had taken root as fact in previous versions of the program. The spinster was so angry that her sister was going to be married before her that she killed the groom-to-be and forged a note to her sister saying he had changed his mind and left town. The younger sister died of a broken heart.

The problem with this story was—and an understanding of the components of a story comes in handy when dealing with local legends—that it did not have a lot of interior logic when you broke it down into "scenes." For example, in the final "scene," the ghost of the younger sister comes back to the house, kills the spinster, and drags her body into a nearby swamp. If both were dead and disappeared into the swamp, who was the witness who passed the story along? In the end the story was merely a collection of well-worn horror clichés about jealously and murder. Many folk songs and tales consist of these same characters and scenes. There was never a pair of sisters named Wade living alone in the house. The confusion arose from the fact that the common practice at the time was to refer to a house by the matriarch's family name. The last name of Earle Webb's mother was Wade.

What was most important in dispelling the myths, however, was good old-fashioned research, which we detail in the next chapter, on the history of the library.

At this point, our investigation of the Webb began in earnest. Joey started paying close attention to the equipment we use during an investigation. A vast array of paranormal investigating equipment is out there, and some engineers and technicians are creating devices that look like something out of *Rocky Horror Picture Show* meets *Brazil*. Combine this with the twenty-first century's natural love of "tech" and the (over) reliance of it on the paranormal shows and it can become a source of confusion and even an obstacle to your investigation to bring too many devices, or to not use them properly.

For the Webb, we found that four pieces of equipment were all we needed. One was the EMF meter. We worked with many inexperienced investigators, so we looked for ways to bring them quickly and visually into the process. The lighting up of an EMF meter got people excited. Of course, during any investigation you need to watch for proximity to smartphones and electrical equipment, both of which will set off EMF meters. As you will see in the chapters to come, the EMF meter was invaluable. We own a pair of the popular K2 EMF meters and have been happy with battery life and reliability.

Another piece of equipment that was helpful at the Webb was a temperature gun. The best ones have both a simple trigger activation and a laser pointer, which comes in handy when ruling out air ducts or the temperature gun pointing at another human being, which might account for temperature fluctuations. The night we auditioned to head the investigations at the Webb, Joey got excited about a temperature rise. It was a little embarrassing when Tonya pointed out that the temperature gun was pointing at Jonathan!

We already mentioned the P-SB11. We have used this "spirit box" in many other places with nowhere near the consistency of communication we obtained at the Webb. Something about the Webb allows the spirits that are drawn to it or reside there to make extensive use of the spirit box. Some of our guest investigators had apps on their smartphones that profess to work like a "spirit box," but we found them unreliable and much too open to interpretation. The ones that bring up a series of words and phrases in text without sound are particularly suspect.

The fourth piece of equipment was a smartphone. We encouraged guest investigators to take pictures quickly and slowly, with the flash on and off, and to use both their video and voice recording features. The facial recognition software on the typical smartphone can also be helpful in identifying the presence of spirits. You will read in the chapters that follow about several instances where this application helped our investigation.

Research is always ongoing, especially when you have the opportunity to investigate a site multiple times. In the case of the Webb, we were there 75 times over the course of two years. As we met new spirits, we sometimes used what they said and how they looked and sounded (their dress, accents, etc.) to do Internet research in real time to find some context about who they were and why they were at the Webb.

A caveat: We kept real-time Internet research to a minimum. We typically had about 90 minutes in the Webb, with a lot of square footage to cover, before the spirits became agitated and asked us to leave. There were a few instances, however, where real-time research was a great help.

After all our investigations of the Webb, Joey always followed up with more thorough research. Sometimes he discovered things to research when he added the case notes from a given night into our database.

We tried out several pieces of equipment during our investigations of the Webb that measure all manner of activity and found them to be mostly unreliable and confusing. Two examples were "Ghost Pumps" (which their designers claim draw spirits to them by sending out an electrical pulse) and three-in-one devices that purportedly measure not only electromagnetic frequencies but also microwaves and radio waves. We experimented with setting up video cameras, which was time consuming and did not yield anything at the Webb. There were a few times when guest investigators brought along cameras and we report on the results in the chapters that follow.

We left as few lights on as possible during our investigations. For some folks who are looking for nothing more than a spooky experience, the near darkness helped to make them feel like they were getting what they came for. There is a much more practical reason for working in low light, with some liquid crystal display (LCD) flashlights to help guide the way. When your eyes are not your main sensing organ, your hearing, sense of smell, and body sensing systems are sharper. This simple technique led to many interesting discoveries and experiences during our time at the Webb, both for us and our guests.

Sharpening the body's senses and sensing systems is an important aspect of our work as paranormal investigators, as well as in Tonya's work as an energy healer and teacher and Joey's work in the theater and in historical–cultural storytelling. Tonya reminded our guests that their bodies were the best piece of equipment they had and that they should trust what they were seeing, hearing, smelling, and feeling and not be shy about vocalizing it as it was happening.

It is also surprising how many guests came to the Webb thinking they had no psychic abilities and within half an hour they were seeing the spirits the way Tonya does. Tonya firmly believes that everyone is born with the ability to sense the subtle energies associated with ghosts and other paranormal events. She feels that the ability to sense these energies, which is often referred to as "psychic" ability, is a natural function of the human body. The degree to which one has these abilities varies. Tonya likens it to athletic or musical ability. Everyone can learn to play a sport or an instrument; however, some people are born with more natural ability to do so and training will sharpen their skills even further.

One reason many people believe they have no "psychic" ability is that they have been conditioned to dismiss any experience for which a "logical" explanation cannot be found. A good example is the experience Tonya had with her Barbie doll when she was five. Unable to find any logic to the situation, her mother quickly dismissed it and insisted Tonya was mistaken about what she'd just seen and experienced. We really can't fault our parents for teaching us to distrust our experiences, as this conditioning is something they most likely experienced from a young age as well.

It is a commonly held belief that babies and small children are able to sense and see things that adults cannot. This is because the young have not been conditioned to believe that what they are seeing isn't "real." The hormonal changes associated with adolescence seem to have a strong effect on these natural abilities, enhancing and returning them to their original state.

This natural ability was most prevalent in teenage girls. On several occasions they immediately described spirits in the Webb exactly the way Tonya saw them, before Tonya said a word. What's most interesting about this is how rarely the girls seemed surprised by this "newfound" ability. It was as if they had always known they had the ability and had simply forgotten it. In an environment in which sharing what they were seeing was not questioned or scorned, they quickly became comfortable accepting their own experiences and freely shared what they were seeing as we moved through the library.

While their mothers were rarely surprised by their newly discovered abilities, their fathers often left after an evening of investigation looking confused and feeling like they got way more than they thought they would. It was fascinating for Joey to watch Tonya mentor people having their first psychic experiences over the course of the evening. Many times we stayed for hours in the parking lot after an investigation helping people make sense of what they experienced and coaching them on how to continue to cultivate their newfound gift.

Of all the advice Tonya shares—both on investigations and with clients—convincing people to trust what they're sensing, feeling, seeing, and experiencing is the most valuable. It is all but impossible to cultivate strong intuitive abilities if you are willing to dismiss what you are experiencing offhand. The urge to trust equipment over one's personal experience is unfortunately quite common, and this is why Tonya says, "Trust what you are sensing! Your body is a much more sophisticated piece of equipment than anything you can buy."

Many people came to the Webb because they had experienced hauntings throughout their lives and were looking for validation and help. The education and practical aspects of how we ran our investigation gave them context, relief, and strategies for managing and understanding their experiences.

There were guests who came to the Webb who were aware of their intuitive or psychic abilities. Some of those guests were happy to share this with the group up front and willingly described what they were sensing and seeing as we moved through the building. Many kept it private. We had several investigations in which, as we were wrapping up at the end, one or more of our guest investigators "confessed" their abilities. These individuals shared a variety of reasons for remaining anonymous throughout the investigation. Usually they were fearful of being scrutinized or questioned. It was encouraging to see how having their experiences validated by Tonya and others in the group (who were seeing and sensing the same things) helped to build confidence for these individuals. There is an unfortunate situation with some mediums where they "test" others who claim the same abilities. Tonya has chosen to be supportive of fellow mediums and sensitives. There is no place for competition here.

The feedback and experiences of the mediums we worked with at the Webb went a long way toward validating what the equipment, research, and Tonya's impressions were telling us. The *clairvoyant* (able to see spirits) or *clairaudient* (able to hear spirits) experiences they shared with us broadened the array of phenomena and heightened even more our appreciation and wonder at what was happening within and outside of the Webb. On every tour, anywhere from one to every guest felt or experienced something.

Pain or pressure in the chest or heart palpitations were perhaps the most prevalent sensations people felt. Given that the first floor was doctors' offices for many years and there were both a hospital and nursing home across the street for decades—and the fact that we met many spirits who exhibited sickness or trauma—this isn't surprising.

Guests, whether knowingly "sensitive" or not, often reported feelings of deep heaviness or sadness throughout the Webb.

In the spirit of responsible investigation, it must be said that the mind is more than ready to play tricks in such an atmosphere as a haunted library paranormal investigation, and there were instances where it was clear that there was either a "groupthink" phenomenon of one person expressing a sensation of being touched, for example, and others in the group quickly latching on to the same, and other times where the atmosphere, stories, and experiences conspired to produce "hackles" and other physical phenomena. It was also very humid on certain nights, with plenty of still air, which could also explain some reports of a feeling of "heaviness."

As investigators it is important to never rule out or dismiss the experience of other investigators, yet it is also important to consider all possibilities. This is where your powers of observation become extremely valuable. The importance of paying close attention to every small detail during an investigation cannot be stressed enough. This is detective work, and every clue is a piece of the puzzle. Over time, we adopted the acronym CAP, which stands for "conditional anomalous phenomena." In other words, we try our best to find mundane, traditionally scientific explanations for what we are experiencing rather than assume it is all paranormal. As the chapters of this book show, however, an impressive number of occurrences passed the CAP test and cannot be easily explained away.

As scientific and objective as we endeavored to be in our ongoing investigation of the Webb Memorial Library, what is truly memorable about our evenings there with our guest investigators was the amount and increasing complexity of the *stories* we were encountering, many of which rivaled any in the action-adventures and thrillers stacked upon the 80-year-old shelves. Because of our background as storytellers, a major component of our investigative style is finding character and story "arcs." For some reason, in the field of paranormal investigation, the larger context is often missing. In many cases getting an EVP (electronic voice phenomena: a recording of a ghostly voice), a spike on the EMF meter, and some shadows on a video camera is more than enough for an investigator. Many travel books and local ghost story collections provide relatively little context to the facts and figures of the person doing the haunting.

In our experience, most hauntings involve former human beings who are now dis-embodied. So, it stands to reason that they all have, in classic story terms, *personalities* that define their character, *motivations* behind why they are at the site and what they are saying and doing, and larger stories of their past (and current) experiences to share. We were fortunate to identify and follow several complex story and character arcs during our time at the Webb. We tracked relationships between the spirits as well as between guests and the spirits. We feel that the details of this work are some of the most interesting sections of this book and that this practice of putting emphasis on story is what makes our work as paranormal investigators unique.

At the end of any investigation we take a few days to let all the collected data—recorded, written in our field notes, and the feedback from guest investigators—sit before we look at it, both in terms of the particular outing and in the larger context of the stories we are following. We make every effort to look at alternative explanations (the CAP test).

In the case of the Webb, these were the air ducts, passing cars on what can be busy streets throwing shadows (especially being a block from the waterfront in a popular summer tourist town), malfunctioning or misused equipment, and the phenomenon of "groupthink."

We also disagree with and challenge each other now and again. We think this is healthy and, given our different skills, genders, and personalities, it gives us a wider array of explanations and possible meanings as to what we are experiencing.

Before we end the chapter, we'd like to mention the necessity of doing research and staying up to date in the field of paranormal research. Aside from watching the paranormal shows, doing Internet research, and subscribing to some of the best-curated databases of paranormal and UFO research (e.g., MUFON), we have an extensive library, with some of our favorite author–researchers being Rosemary Ellen Guiley, Nick Redfern, Stan Gordon, Gray Barker, John Keel, Graham Phillips, and Andrew Collins. We also listen to *Coast to Coast AM* and other podcasts and try to attend conferences and festivals a few times a year.

When you consider how broad the field of the paranormal is—from crypto-zoology (Bigfoot, Mothman), cattle mutilations, psychic questing, and UFOs/MIBs (Men in Black) to ghosts, residual hauntings, poltergeists, and demonic entities—no one can be an expert at everything. Knowing an array of experts that you can go to for photographic analysis, case studies, and to explore theories with is a necessity in order to be responsible investigators. As we said, we are always looking for *context*—the combinations and conditions that come together to allow for hauntings.

A working knowledge of quantum physics is necessary to make sense of some of the instances related in this book where linear time and space as we know them through traditional science seemed to break down at the Webb, as they did when we encountered the interdimensional in Point Pleasant, West Virginia in 2009.

Tonya also feels that learning to tune into your body's natural sensing systems in order to allow yourself to become a receiver for the energetic information that surrounds you is vitally important. In addition, learning about the human energy system through exploration of practices such as meditation, energy work, and yoga can go a long way toward helping develop your natural psychic abilities. The human energy system is your interface with the subtle energies behind paranormal experiences, so a basic understanding of these energies will serve to expand your awareness.

An understanding of these energies serves another important function during investigations. Protection. Everything that exists in the universe is made up of energy vibrating at different frequencies. Energies that vibrate at a higher frequency are associated with positive effects and feelings. Experiences such as love, laughter, and bliss are good examples of higher-vibrating frequencies. Fear and anger vibrate at much lower frequencies. Spirits are attracted to and "feed" on the energies of the living. When investigating haunted locations, it is important to keep your energy vibration high, to avoid "feeding" and attracting malevolent entities and spirits. Tonya has learned this the hard way. On occasions that she allowed herself to give into fear, her encounters and experiences with various entities were undesirable. On a few of these occasions she had entities follow her home and make threatening contact with her through dreams. On occasions when she refused to allow her fear to take over, Tonya made contact with many benevolent, even comedic, personalities. You'll meet many of them in this book.

It is important to understand your intentions before commencing your investigation. Why are you there? What is it that you hope to learn, experience, prove, and/or accomplish? If you participate in an investigation from a place of sincere curiosity and approach the spirits you encounter with compassion and respect, you are likely to have a more positive and productive experience than if your only intention going in is thrill-seeking and provocation. Like anything worth doing, being a good paranormal investigator requires a great deal of self-development and self-examination.

All this can be daunting, and you want to have all the tools at your disposal that you can.

As you will see in the chapters to come, we believe that synchronicity (Jung's "acausal connecting principle" or, as most folks know it—coincidence or serendipity) does have a place in paranormal research, and we provide a few of the best, most relevant examples we encountered at the Webb in this book.

We revisit the components of our investigating style in the final chapter, "Get the Information Out There: What We've Learned and How it Applies to Paranormal Investigation Beyond the Webb," through a slightly different lens, presenting them as a checklist of sorts for others in the field, based on what we've learned so far.

3
Monumental but Not Pompous
A History of the Webb Memorial Library

The Webb Memorial Library is located in Morehead City, Carteret County, on the "Crystal Coast" of North Carolina. Surrounded by historic towns rich in pirate and other maritime history and lore, Morehead City is a combination tourist town and, with its four-lane Highway 70, a busy commercial corridor that features a broad array of restaurants, shops, and boutiques.

The Webb is located on Ninth Street, in the older part of town, not far from a bustling commercial port. While the towns around it, such as Beaufort, were founded in the early 1700s, Morehead City was not founded until 1857. It boasts the start of a railroad that once extended all the way to San Diego, California.

In the mid-1850s, the former governor of North Carolina, John Motley Morehead, and Silas Webb (the owner of a general store on the lot where the Webb would be built and the grandfather of the man who built the Webb Memorial Library) visited Beaufort's port and harbor, not far from where the infamous Blackbeard sank his flagship, the *Queen*

Anne's Revenge, in 1718. They quickly determined that the area that would become Morehead City was perfect for a larger port because of its deep water and easy access, a combination all too rare on the treacherous Crystal Coast. Morehead was also responsible for getting the railroad funded, which led to increased tourism and more success for the fishing industry that is an economic lynchpin of the area.

As tourism grew following the Civil War, the opulent Atlantic Hotel was built in 1880 and quickly became a destination for wealthy socialites and those wanting to summer at the beach. Boasting almost 300 rooms, the Atlantic Hotel had every amenity imaginable. Although it struggled through the years of the First World War and a flu pandemic, The Atlantic Hotel survived beyond its heyday, until on April 15, 1933, fishermen noticed smoke coming from the resort and within an hour it had burned to the ground. It was never rebuilt.

Five years before the fire at the Atlantic Hotel, only blocks away, Silas's grandson, Earle Webb Sr., purchased the two lots where his childhood home used to sit and began plans for a multi-use, two-story, Federal-style building that would make his hometown better for its residents, who were just feeling the effects of the Great Depression. Having grown up in Morehead City, and staying at the Atlantic Hotel when he visited from his home and offices in New York, Earle Webb Sr. had made quite the success of himself and wanted to give something back. After earning his law degree at the University of Michigan, he rose to the position of general counsel for General Motors. In 1925 he became chief executive officer of the Ethyl Corporation, a collaboration between General Motors and Standard Oil of New Jersey, with manufacturing handled by Dupont. Called "monumental but not pompous" and "a great man" by those he worked with, Webb saved the Ethyl Corporation from ruin.

The Webb building was not originally a library. The offices of Dr. Benjamin Franklin Royal and Dr. Sanford "Sam" Webb Thompson Jr. were downstairs and there was a training facility for the Morehead City Garment Company upstairs. Both doctors play a prominent role in the history of the Webb, both physically and in spirit. Dr. Thompson, who is a main character in the chapters that follow, sold one of the two lots to Mr. Webb, and Dr. Royal was instrumental in building the hospital across the street and running the burn unit there during World War II. The hospital and burn unit also contribute to the haunted history of the Webb.

When the Morehead City Garment Company's new plant was complete, the training facility relocated. Its manager may have stayed behind as a spirit, however, as we discuss in the chapters on the second floor. Earle's wife, Eva, who was a member of the Morehead Woman's Club, arranged for their lending library (approximately 300 volumes) to be moved to the second floor.

A few years later, the Webbs' son, Earle W. Webb Jr., became ill with a lung infection while visiting during the holidays, and died. He was 19 years old. In 1936, after extensive remodeling, the grieving Webbs rededicated the building as the Earle W. Webb Jr. Memorial Library and Civic Center, opening its doors to local citizens for community use.

The Webbs continued to know tragedy in the years to come. In 1941 Eva died, and in 1944 their son Arnold was killed in a boating accident on the Neuse River in North Carolina.

In 2003, the trust supporting the facility was no longer viable. As of this writing, the library's board of directors is still in the process of exploring options so that it can continue to serve the community. In 2013 an elevator was installed in accordance with the Americans with Disabilities Act, which may have further charged the paranormal activity.

Despite their emotional ties to the property and building, we never encountered one of the deceased Webbs during our time investigating the Webb Memorial Library.

4
It's Me

Ninth and Evans Streets and the Courtyard

It was always with a bit of healthy nervousness that we awaited our guest investigators on any given night outside the Webb. Over time, we settled into a routine that helped to steady our nerves and get us ready mentally and energetically for the experiences to come.

First, why the nerves? The Haunted Webb Memorial "tour" was a publicly advertised opportunity for people to participate in a real, ongoing paranormal investigation, and we never knew what to expect as far as attendees and group dynamics. Over the course of the two years that we were the lead investigators, we met the curious, the skeptical, the cynical, the surprised (they either misunderstood what the tour involved or someone booked it for them and kept it a secret until the last minute), the frightened, pranksters, the bored, a few drunken bachelorette parties, a drunken birthday party, and those who were paranormal enthusiasts. Our youngest investigator was 13 years old (his father dropped him off with his two brothers and offered us extra money—which we declined— to scare him [we didn't]) and our oldest were in their early 80s.

After centering ourselves, visualizing white light, and calling upon our spirit guides for insight and protection, our routine consisted of walking the perimeter of the property with an EMF meter and sometimes the P-SB11 to get a sense of the energy emanating from the building. We often spent some time in the courtyard, a fenced-in area with benches, a fountain, several plant beds, and a freestanding wooden archway perfect for wedding vows. We also took a series of pictures of the building, focusing on a few windows in particular for reasons detailed in this chapter. Joey made sure the rest of the equipment and the flashlights were all in working order. Spirits can be hard on batteries and on the equipment in general, which generally kept him busy throughout the night.

The courtyard.

As the guest investigators arrived, we asked them about where they were from, what their experiences with the paranormal were, and what their expectations of the evening might be. Then we took them to the courtyard, which was where we did our welcome speech and gave the group an abbreviated version of the chapter you just read so they had historical context for some of what they were going to experience.

On many nights the spirits could not wait until we were inside to begin communicating. The rest of this chapter details those encounters.

Ninth and Evans Streets

The main entrance to the library is on Ninth Street. This is where the parking spaces are, and where we gathered as the guests arrived. Evans Street runs parallel to Hwy 70 and is where the previous hospital—now the Bask Hotel and the remaining wing of the nursing home that took over the hospital—once stood.

We had not been investigating the Webb for long before Tonya noticed a man in a seersucker suit on Ninth Street. She also saw him by a tree by the former hospital on Evans. Although he changed location and she saw him walking the street at times, he never acknowledged us or communicated in any way.

There were numerous occasions when guests in the first floor rooms that face Ninth and Evans saw both male and female spirits. Tonya saw two women through the Evans Street windows.

One night, as we were gathering on Ninth Street, two teenage guests saw a lady's face in a second floor window.

Not all the presences outside the Webb were human. A "ghost kitty" was reported by a medium who joined us one night, and Tonya once saw a black shape on the roof. A moment later, she saw activity in the same window where the two teenage guests reported seeing the lady's face.

The black shape on the roof of the Webb is interesting because, some weeks later, Joey was doing an investigation with someone he had known for a long time, who was training as his backup. Before anyone arrived, they took a photo on Ninth Street with the Webb to their backs to post on Facebook with Joey's iPhone 4. They were surprised to see a black mass between them when they looked at the picture, which neither they nor several paranormal investigators they sent the photo to could explain.

Although we never encountered the spirits of the Webbs, a medium who was beginning his training with us was at the entrance on Ninth Street his first night and said he sensed the death of a son. Just beyond that door, in the main entrance, is a portrait of Earle Webb Jr.

Several investigators were unable to explain the shadow between Joey and fellow investigator Robby Justiss. It has a very similar shape to the interdimensional shown on page 125.

In June 2017 we were testing the equipment when we heard a male voice on the P-SB11. It was a man named Justin. Tonya asked him if he wanted to come into the Webb with us. He asked, "Here?" and said, "Tonya."

Tonya saw a vision of a boating accident. We heard a woman's voice and Tonya saw her standing with Justin. Tonya invited them to come in. She felt that they had a message to share. In the hallway on the first floor later that night we heard "Justin" and "Authority." We checked the newspapers in one of the first floor rooms at Justin's request at the end of the investigation. There was an article about a boating accident and another about someone named Justin, but no evidence that either was related to the two spirits we met in the parking lot (one of the truths about paranormal investigation is that *coincidence* does not equal *correlation* in most instances). We never heard from Justin and the woman again.

A week later, Joey turned on the P-SB11 in the parking lot before the tour and heard, "Headshot," "Fuck you," "Pick up," and "Ron." Several weeks after that initial communication, Ron made himself known to us on the second floor of the Webb in an intriguing and perhaps space-time-defying encounter you will read about in later chapters.

The morning after an investigation where we encountered a good bit of hostility from some of the spirits, a guest emailed to say that while we were in the courtyard he had looked into a first floor window and saw an angry old woman staring at him through the glass.

For months we tracked moon phases, temperature, and weather to see if certain conditions increased activity. We found no clear correlations. That said, on Halloween night 2017 we had the opportunity to do a special lecture on our investigative techniques and lead a two-and-a-half-hour investigation (investigations are typically 90 minutes).

Things certainly amped up from the moment we got out of the car. The building was almost pulsating with energy. We could feel it in our nervous systems and the hair on our arms was standing up. As guests arrived, they could also feel it.

Throughout the chapters to come you will read about our experiences that memorable Halloween night.

The Courtyard

As people passed through the wrought iron gate that leads to the courtyard, we felt a change in their energy, in their breathing. It was not "spooky" per se, but the low light coming from a lone electric lamppost that looked like the old gas lamps of the late nineteenth century and the rhythmic babble of the fountain conspired to change the mood to one of quiet attention. While we related the history of the building and the Webbs, guests invariably started taking pictures of the courtyard and the building. There is a window on the second floor that drew many people's attention. We called it "Vincent's window" after the spirit who occupied it and the northern hallway for over a year. One of our guest investigators who came to the Webb more than once, Michelle W., captured a ghostly figure in it one night.

Sensitives, upon entering the courtyard, immediately reported feeling eyes on them from that window, but their interpretations were on a wide continuum. Some felt as though the intent behind the stare

Image of a face taken from the courtyard (photo courtesy Michelle Williams).

was menacing and others felt as though an old friend was happy to see them. Some of the returning guests were remembered by the spirits. This applied to us as well. We often heard our names or the names of returning guests through the P-SB11.

On a particularly active night we heard a female voice say, "Welcome." Tonya saw a female form just after. We also heard, "Joey," "What's up, man?" and "Hello." Some days later we had a guest who identified herself as a medium at the start of the evening tell us that she was being escorted into the Webb by a spirit named John who followed her into the room where we did our introductions. The chapter about the "Cannon Room" relates our interactions with a spirit named John who used modern phrases like the "What's up, man?" we had heard days before. We are confident that it was he who escorted the medium in.

Female spirits far outnumbered male spirits in the courtyard. During an early investigation, in the northwest corner of the courtyard, Tonya got a flash image of a young woman and heard in her head the name "Jessica." At a bistro table in the courtyard months later, Tonya saw an image of a little girl with black hair, bangs, and a big red bow, perhaps named Eva. There was no reason to believe that this was in any way related to Eva Webb. Sensitives also reported seeing a lady in a white dress who was usually inside what we called the Back Stacks on the first floor. There was also a man seen by a teenage medium.

Upon our arrival at the Webb one night in December 2016, our instinct was to scan the courtyard with the EMF meter and P-SB11 before a special private party of two guest investigators arrived. We had a feeling this would be an interesting night. These two guests were so motivated to experience the Webb they had paid for three extra tickets so that the investigation could meet its financial requirements. The spirits at the Webb respond to the genuinely curious and respectful the same way living people do—with much more talkative and animated interactions. The experiences we had that night are related in the chapters to come.

Vincent, staring out from his window, said through the P-SB11, "It's me." We also detected the presence of another male spirit, who identified himself as Dwight and said "Sixteen." EMF spikes at the freestanding archway and near the fountain were in the middle range (orange on the K2).

In the next chapter, you will meet the spirit of a young boy in suspenders and a "newsboy cap" that Tonya named "Oliver." Although it was rare for child spirits to be seen on the second floor, Oliver was occupying that same window one evening.

On a night in May 2017, during a time when a group of angry male spirits were congregating on the second floor, we arrived earlier than usual and took extra time walking around the exterior of the building. At the far end of the courtyard, near the archway, we sensed an unsettling energy. We also noticed that the electric lamppost in the courtyard was out. When we asked the person who handled our scheduling and communications with the Webb about it the next day we found out there had been ongoing and puzzling trouble with the electricity outside the building. It is our feeling that the male spirits upstairs did not want us assembling in the courtyard. The active second floor window is near the area where they had been gathering. They did not want to be seen or interacted with. The chapters that relate our experiences on the second floor with these spirits from spring to autumn 2017 detail many examples of their attempts to prevent us from being certain places and asking questions of the spirits in the Webb.

The courtyard was busy one night in August 2017. Tonya and a sensitive who was training to join our investigative team both saw what they described as a garden tea party.

The courtyard also generated considerable synchronicities. Here is one of the most compelling. Despite having approximately 500 guests over the course of more than 70 investigations, Lily Dale Assembly, New York, the famous training center for mediums, was only mentioned once. On the date that it was mentioned, by a guest who had just visited there, Joey had spent several hours earlier in the day researching Lily Dale for a screenplay he had been commissioned to write about the real-life experiences of the youngest medium ever trained at the center and her family. What makes this synchronicity all the more interesting is that the family of mediums upon which the screenplay is based had a strong connection to John and Tim Frick and Point Pleasant (see the Prologue)—a fact that we did not realize until weeks *after* Joey had been hired to write the screenplay.

In the winter of 2018 Tonya captured a few ghostly images on her cell phone from a window in what we call the Introduction Room overlooking the courtyard. By way of due diligence and the CAP ("conditional anomalous phenomena") test, we experimented by having people sit opposite the window to check for reflections while Joey stood in the courtyard looking in the window so Tonya could make comparisons. As he stood at the window, he held the P-SB11 beyond the boundary of the window. A male voice said, "Nutty." When Tonya came outside he told her what he heard. She laughed and said she was acting nutty while taking the pictures—singing and talking to herself about "ghosteses" because she was nervous about being in the room alone.

One last thing about the courtyard before we take you inside the Webb, room by room, hallway by hallway, as we did our guest investigators. The Webb has three exterior doors, all of which use the same key. Unless the lights were out in the courtyard, making it hard to navigate, we always entered the building through its door. Starting in early summer of 2017 and lasting several weeks, it often took Joey three tries to get the key to fit into the lock. It was as though the lock shrank or the key swelled just enough that the key would not slide into it. Invariably, after three tries, the key went in without difficulty.

Image of a man outside the window of the Introduction Room.

It is understandable that some of the spirits would not want us to enter the building—especially the group of angry males that were making their presence known in force when the key difficulties first began happening. But—and this is one of the mysteries of the Webb that kept us going back—it also happened as we were leaving. Three tries, no luck. Then the key would suddenly fit the lock.

This experience of "three tries" to open a lock may sound familiar. If so, it's because it happens frequently in folklore and fairy tales—along with "three wishes," "knocking three times," "thrice times the charm," and so on. As a matter of fact, it is so prevalent in storytelling that writers call the practice of repeating key actions, rituals, or themes three times "the Rule of Three." When you consider that folklore, fairy tales, and myths are our oldest stories, refined over thousands of years and millions of tellings, based on humankind's most primal experiences, the lock only working after three tries is probably not coincidence.

47

5
Take My Picture
The Introduction Room

As we moved through the courtyard door into a small space that led to the door of the Introduction Room (hereafter the Intro Room; we did our introduction to how the investigation would proceed and how to use the equipment there), it was interesting to watch the faces and feel the energy of the guests. Although the Webb is not "spooky" in the Gothic sense, it is nearly 100 years old and full of dark wood trim and many pieces of antique furniture. There was no light when we first entered and the hallway off the courtyard entrance had a bit of an "off kilter" feel to it.

The Intro Room had bookshelves on each of its walls and a square reading area with two wingback chairs and a couch with a coffee table in the center. There was a combination schoolhouse-style desk and chair that probably dates from the early 1900s and a child-sized rocking chair.

What did (or did not) happen in the Intro Room usually set the tone for the night's investigation. During an investigation in February 2018 the EMF meters were all cycling from green to red over and over as we did our introduction. We heard the sound of blues piano, as if it was

49

The Introduction Room.

coming from the other side of the first floor. That night turned out to be one of the most active we experienced.

As part of the introduction, Tonya went over the rules, which we kept simple: (1) it is a working library, so things should be treated with respect and not unnecessarily moved or handled; (2) no gum chewing, food, or drinks; (3) stay with the group (this became even more important after some instances of investigators being scratched or pushed while alone in a room during an investigation); (4) do not enter rooms that have their doors closed; (5) the spirits are not to be disrespected, yelled at, insulted, or provoked (this was a response to some of the poor practices shown on some "reality" paranormal shows). At times we got pushback on rule five. If the guests were adamant about "riling up" the spirits, Joey let them know that the investigation would end if they attempted it. We never had to go that far. A gentle reminder was sometimes needed and was always heeded.

The third rule—not separating from the group—was important to ensure the integrity of the investigation. We set up game pieces or dolls in some rooms to see if they moved over the course of the night, as they did on occasion (see the chapters on the Children's Room and Cannon Room). We made sure not to be the last or first ones into the room and that everyone was accounted for. Unfortunately, on a few nights, guests either out for some fun or testing our integrity as researchers tried to trick us by sneaking away and moving items around the room.

Part of the introduction was letting guests know the three types of entities they might encounter at the Webb. The first, which was rare (one instance each on the first and second floors), was a "residual haunting." Joey explained this as akin to taking a short length of film, usually containing a single action, and playing it on a loop.

In one of the wingback chairs in the Intro Room there was, for about a year, a sad, sobbing woman dressed all in black. In the first eight months of our investigation, guests almost nightly picked up on her emotion—especially if they were sitting in "her chair." We got a variety of responses from the guests—some felt sad, some exhausted, and one woman said that her throat hurt as if she had been crying.

Since the Intro Room was part of the doctors' suites, we surmise that this was a woman from the first half of the 1930s who received bad news from one of the doctors about either herself or a loved one. As time went on, fewer guests sensed her and by March 2017, she was no longer there.

There was a residual haunting in what we called the Portal Hallway (Chapter 12).

Another type of entity was nonhuman. We encountered black mists and blobs, wraithlike figures, and at least one interdimensional. Details are provided in the chapters correlating to where they were seen.

The third type of entity was by far the most prevalent: Disembodied spirits of former human beings. Or, as Tonya likes to refer to them, "people without bodies."

The boy spirit Oliver showed up in the Intro Room about once a month. He was often sitting at the schoolhouse desk. One night he was in the courtyard waiting for us. When we entered the Intro Room, "his" rocking chair was in the middle of the floor. Oliver was attracted to the EMF meters. During the introduction Joey arranged all the equipment on the coffee table, and Tonya on several occasions saw Oliver reaching for it.

Other children showed themselves in the Intro Room. One night there was a little boy, dressed in modern Bermuda shorts and a plaid shirt, sitting in the child-sized rocking chair. Two sensitives felt like they were going to cry. He was still there two weeks later. We never got a name or discerned any part of his story.

Tonya also saw a teenage cheerleader in red and white in that room.

A night in late June 2016 proved to be eventful and exciting. We were joined by two groups of guest investigators that had sensitives among them. At the start of the investigation, everyone was gathered in the Intro Room and heavy footsteps were heard in the hallway. All the investigators were inside the room and there was no one in the hallway when the footsteps were heard.

Communication from the P-SB11 was unclear and garbled, and we weren't making anything out until a sensitive asked Tonya if she was wearing perfume. Tonya replied that she was wearing an essential oil (she did not say which one), immediately after which the word "Rosemary" was clearly heard through the P-SB11. Tonya jumped with surprise because the essential oil she was wearing *was* rosemary!

In mid-April 2017, everyone heard what sounded like carnival/ organ music from upstairs. A few of the guests and Joey also heard what can be described as an old Walter Cronkite–style network news broadcast. Tonya went upstairs to play the piano to see if that was what we had heard. It was not. As Tonya came back down, she saw a spirit in the hallway dressed like a clown that she had seen on prior visits. Her sense was that this was a human spirit who knew she dislikes clowns, so he was messing with her.

In mid-May 2017, in the Art Section of the Intro Room, between a set of books roughly 18 inches wide, the EMF meters registered in the middle range (orange). The same occurred on July 7. The area where the EMF spiked orange expanded another foot (six inches in each direction) by July 20 and the area remained the same on August 2, sometimes spiking red. The area of activity shrank several inches on August 4 and expanded again to its original range by the end of the month. The area had shrunk and weakened in early September. By Friday, October 13, the activity had ceased, although it returned to a three-book span in February 2018. We were not able to discern what caused the activity beyond a correlation with the timing of when the activity upstairs with the angry male spirits was strongest.

One night on the P-SB11 we heard a series of communications, including "Jack," "Dr. Brown?" and "Why don't you try——?" We were unable to locate any documentation linking a "Jack" or "Dr. Brown" to the offices at the Webb. On a different evening the temperature gauge on the P-SB11 increased and we heard, "Take my picture." Several guests took pictures around the room but no spirits were visible in any of the photos.

In late August we met the spirit of an African American girl named Verna in the Intro Room. She was playful and happy. When we returned to the room later in the evening she played with Tonya's hair. She followed us home and appeared in a dream to a medium who was part of the investigation that night. They were having a picnic together. She was seen by another medium in the Intro Room a week later.

In late August 2017, a guest felt a pull across the library and back into the Intro Room about 20 minutes into the investigation. There were two male spirits in there that set the EMF meters into the red and registered a temperature increase on the gauge built into the P-SB11. (Joey theorizes that the temperature *increases* on the P-SB11, which is opposite of what we expect from the presence of a spirit, because the spirits, in their efforts to communicate through the box, heat up the components and battery.)

The Intro Room is an area where two of the mediums on our investigative team were physically injured by spirits. In both instances, they were separated from the group. Jolie was shoved into a piece of furniture by the spirit of an old man she described as having "crazy white hair." This could have been the spirit of a former patient/resident of either the hospital or the nursing home. A week later, Bryon, a medium who joined our investigation in mid-2017, was drawn into the Intro Room while the group was elsewhere on the first floor, and was scratched on the middle of his back. Joey saw three parallel scratches about four and a half inches long on his back. This was the first evidence we witnessed of spirits leaving physical marks on someone's body, although we had heard stories of this happening several years prior during an earlier incarnation of the Webb tour.

We always ended our investigation back in the Intro Room, where we did a debriefing and took questions. We had several interesting experiences during that time.

As we started packing up one night, the EMF meters flashed red and blinked on and off in synch to "yes" and "no" questions the guests were asking. In the fall of 2017, we had an experience where the spirits did things to keep us from leaving (although we did still get requests for us to leave on some nights, as you will read about in the chapters on the second floor). Tonya saw the spirit of a little boy digging around in a medium's camera bag. She sensed there was a toy or something fun in the bag. She was right—there was a bottle of bubbles! The medium opened the bottle and set it on the floor for the boy to play with.

As the group walked down the hall to the Intro Room to wrap up on a different night, a girl's voice was heard from the P-SB11. The voice said, "Wait" and "Don't," and the temperature dropped according to the gauge on the spirit box. There was also the sound of a child's laughter as we entered the room. As we said, it was unusual for any spirit to ask us to wait by that time of the evening.

Joey had half a dozen experiences with clairaudience in the Webb. When we went back into the Intro Room one night, he heard steps going upstairs and two girls' voices.

Once, while putting away the equipment in the Intro Room, an EMF meter flashed green, *although it was turned off.* We had other anomalies with the equipment in that room. At the end of September 2016, the P-SB11 and temperature gun *spontaneously switched on* as Joey took them out of the equipment bag at the start of the evening. That night was particularly active throughout the Webb. It was as though the spirits could not wait to let us know they were there.

In December 2017 we were joined by a female guest who was fearful the whole night. After the introduction she had said, "I don't know if I can do this." At the end of the night, as we returned to the Intro Room, she put the EMF meter down and it spiked to solid red, freaking her out. Joey asked the spirit if it was "time to go." The EMF meter ran up the color scale, from green to red, three times. Joey said, "If you want us to go, as a sign, please stop setting off the EMF meter." It did. We left.

We close this chapter with one of the oddest stories we were a part of at the Webb. Two sensitives were participating in the investigation one night without identifying themselves as such. Based on their reactions and comments, as we settled into the Intro Room at the end of the night, Joey asked if they were sensitives. One said that she was and that she lived in a "creepy" house. The other sensitive agreed. Dr. Thompson entered the room and showed Tonya the spirit of an old lady who fancies herself a witch. The description fit with what the woman sensed in her house. The sensitive that owned the house said she thought the witch spirit had killed her pet bird. Tonya got an image of the bird, describing it almost perfectly, and saw the witch spirit push a long needle into its chest, performing some sort of ritual magic and killing it.

With that bit of news, we ended the investigation.

6
Hi There
The Elevator and First Floor Hallway

As we exited into the hallway from the Intro Room, we would feel an increase in the excitement and anticipation. Guests shone their small LCD flashlights down the main hallway, anticipating what they might see or feel. Some took pictures.

Our first stop in the hallway was the elevator, which was installed in 2013. Any type of construction can be traumatic for the spirits who inhabit a space. Investigators often report in the paranormal literature about renovations stirring spirits up. It is nothing less than an intrusion, disruption, and an unwanted change. This is one explanation for why the Webb is so active. Elevators in particular cause a lot of trauma to a building, requiring a lot of tearing out of the old and creating a new infrastructure over, in this instance, two floors. For the benefit of the guests, Joey likened it to sitting quietly in your room, journaling or listening to music with headphones when a wrecking ball comes through the wall. Your response won't be small.

In the case of the Webb, it did not take anything as traumatic as the installation of an elevator to create unwanted change for the spirits within its walls. In the last two weeks of April 2018, just days before we delivered this book to the publisher, we returned to the Webb four times after a month away. Two of the spirits who consistently communicated with us were out of sorts the first night of our return because there had been so many changes made in our absence. There was new, modern furniture in one of the rooms and another room had its lighting changed. Changes in room layout, electrical outlets, and placement of furniture continued through the end of April and the spirits became increasingly uncommunicative. We could feel a substantial change in the energy.

When we first began the Webb investigation, in May 2016, it was part of the itinerary to bring guests into the elevator a few at a time, to experience its considerable orb activity. Orbs, usually paired, moving rapidly from floor to ceiling on an almost perfect vertical axis, were photographed and video recorded on numerous occasions. The EMF meters also spiked on some nights, but not consistently, so we do not believe the elevator was the cause.

Cell phones and cameras at times stopped working all together, or only when held in a certain way (one night, a camera stopped operating when held at a 35-degree angle), but when the guests stepped out of the elevator, the equipment worked fine.

As interesting as the orbs were, by September 2016 we talked about the elevator but did not take guests inside, for two reasons. First, so much activity happened elsewhere in the Webb by that time and bringing guests into the elevator two or three at a time (with 15–20 of them in the group) became too time consuming. Second, the space was cramped, even with three people. One night Joey inadvertently hit the police call button on the panel behind him. A dispatcher spoke through the elevator speaker and asked what the emergency was. Joey explained we were doing a tour and the button had been hit accidentally. We thought that was the end of it.

A few minutes later, as Tonya stood in the hallway with the guests waiting their turn in the elevator, there was a loud knock at the far end. Everyone jumped. Tonya started down the hallway to investigate and asked if anyone wanted to join her. No one volunteered. As she continued down the pitch-black hallway (she doesn't carry a flashlight) she heard the knock again and realized it was coming from the Ninth Street door. She was getting nervous. Tonya unlocked the door as she heard a much louder knock. Opening the door, she found a tall police officer. A nervous laugh of relief echoed through the hallway as she exclaimed, "You scared the crap outta me!" The policeman chuckled and indicated that he had to follow up on the emergency call button as a matter of procedure.

We stopped going into the elevator soon after.

On occasion, guests sensed anger and aggression in front of the elevator. The strangest thing that occurred with the elevator happened one night in late summer 2017. While we were on the second floor, we thought we heard the elevator moving. When we went back downstairs later in the evening, we confirmed it. The elevator had been on the second floor when we started the investigation (the bright red "2" is hard to miss in the dark hallway) and now it was a bright red "1."

The rest of this chapter highlights our experiences in the first floor hallway, moving from north to south.

Joey entered the building one night before the investigation to turn off a front hallway light that the library staff had left on and felt a heaviness in the air in the first floor that did not often occur. As we did the introduction a guest noticed a shadow block the light at the far end of the first floor. We investigated. Several investigators noticed a large black form by the front door and reported sensations of dizziness and an overall heaviness. One guest intuited that the spirit was inviting us to stay, as if it wanted our prolonged attention. A shadow was seen from the Intro Room in the same place in February 2018.

Tonya saw a male spirit dressed as a clown holding balloons just outside the Intro Room on several occasions. Once, it was right after Joey and a guest both saw a bright blue orb the size of a grapefruit float past the open door. There were other reports of blue lights on the first floor that night.

In December 2017 our daughter, Jolie, who is also a talented medium who has seen spirits since she was a toddler (see Chapter 1), saw a figure outside the Intro Room. All she could see was a white human-shaped mass—which followed us everywhere we went on the first floor. It followed us home and wreaked havoc in our kitchen for a week (cracking an egg sitting on the counter, snapping the plastic handle of a milk jug in the refrigerator, putting a bread tie in the oven while it was on, and spilling things) and then knocking things over in Jolie's room before revealing itself to be a mischievous 16-year-old boy in overalls and a Henley shirt.

The two temperature guns dropped 10 degrees as we walked toward the staircase at the midway point of the hallway one night and we heard, "Hi there" on the P-SB11. By the stairs a spirit that Tonya and other mediums believed to be a former librarian who seemed to be in charge of things downstairs said, "Now think about this." We were unsure as to what she was referring. Perhaps it was the investigation in general, or it was an echo of some past lecture she gave to an employee or patron. We heard male voices say, "Buddy" and "Stay up."

Another night, in that same area, we heard through the P-SB11, "Get the information out there." Joey replied, "We are." The response was, "Great!" At the end of another night Joey said, "Let's go into the Intro Room." On the P-SB11, in a sing-song voice, we heard, "Into the Intro Room!"

Next to the stairs are the doors to the basement and ladies' room. In the space between them, two of our guest investigators felt their skin tingling, and the hair on their arms and necks stood up. Another guest complained it was difficult to breathe while standing there. We moved from the hallway into the ladies' room and immediately noted a 13-degree drop in temperature that could not be accounted for from air conditioning. The P-SB11 was emitting several distinct voices; we were unable to make out what was being said.

While in the Intro Room one night, Joey heard something being moved in the hallway by the front door. When we moved to the area by the stairs some time later, Joey realized it was a stepstool on wheels. Through clairaudience, he heard a nearby male voice say, "Go away." See the section on the men's room in Chapter 8 for information on who this spirit might be.

Many people heard footsteps in the first floor hallway, or the creaking of the wooden floorboards, while in the Intro or Children's rooms.

One evening, a light was on in the locked room across from the Intro Room. Joey asked if anyone had noticed if it was on when we entered. From the P-SB11 we heard, "Yes." Another evening a guest watched a lamp at the end of the hallway switch on and off.

Near the end of one evening's investigation, we headed downstairs when we all heard a sound down the hall toward the Intro Room. We heard a male voice on the P-SB11 say, "Wait a minute." Joey asked if the spirit wanted us to stay and he said, "Yup." At that moment a guest heard an "old style" doorknob turn several times (the guest meant a doorknob with a long stem and a glass or porcelain knob). We went to investigate and found the basement door closed but unlatched. Its doorknob was "old style." A guest and Tonya both said that while they were near the bathroom door, a few feet from the basement door, earlier in the night, they had both looked at the basement door and it had been latched.

After the investigation ended the guest reported to us that before he heard the doorknob he saw a silhouette of a person about three feet high wearing a short-brimmed hat in the hallway. This matched the description of the spirit of the boy Tonya affectionately called Oliver.

Outside the Children's Room in September 2016 the temperature gauge on the P-SB11 went to blue, registering an unprecedented drop of three degrees (the maximum the meter reads) and we heard, "Fuck you." (The drop in temperature on the P-SB11 gauge that causes the indicator to shine blue correlated in the Webb with hostile spirits. We also had the indicator go to blue in one of the igloos in Point Pleasant in the TNT area during an encounter with a dark entity.)

Tonya saw a female spirit in mid-August 2017 pointing upstairs. There were several incidents upstairs that night.

Batteries drained quickly in the Webb, especially in the P-SB11. On average, a heavy duty nine-volt lasted a maximum of two hours and 15 minutes. Sometimes we had to change the battery every 90 minutes. One evening in December 2016, Joey went downstairs to replace the P-SB11 battery (having neglected to put a spare in his pocket), he noticed that the interior door by the circulation desk entrance was open at a 90-degree angle. There was a Christmas tree made of paperback books and an easel with a poster for an interesting event that he had read prior to going upstairs, so he would have noticed if the door was open (the area is small and it would be hard to get past it). Another guest had been in the area as well and agreed the door had not been open.

Sixteen months later we were in the Intro Room and six people heard the sound of wind chimes by the foyer by that door. Joey went to investigate. There was nothing in the area that could make that sound.

As he explored with his flashlight he heard two knocks from the door, which was open behind him. They made enough vibration to rattle a bracket hanging from the top of the door. When he went back into the Intro Room the guests asked, "Did you hear two knocks?"

Right beside the front foyer is the circulation area, a section we generally avoided because of all the electronics (e.g., printers, phones, a dozen computers), although it would sometimes make itself impossible to ignore. In May 2016 a group had a strong sense of an angry energy in a corner behind the circulation desk, which dissipated within a few moments of our acknowledging it.

On another occasion, two of our investigators observed lights in the circulation area, similar to an orb observed there by an investigator two weeks earlier. In October 2017 we heard a name that started with C (we have chosen not to give the full name). One of the library's staff was on the investigation that night and thought the spirit was referring to a long-time champion of the library who had died 18 months earlier. It could be that she came through because he was there. Later that evening the library employee was holding an EMF meter that spiked to red for several straight minutes. Tonya saw a big, imposing man standing near him. When we entered the courtyard to go home, the imposing spirit followed, continuing to spike the EMF meter.

On a night in late March 2017, near the circulation desk, a female voice spoke a friendly "Hello" on the P-SB11. A medium also sensed a male in a position of authority, who was perhaps a past library administrator. Tonya sensed that he liked to be called "Mister" and that he was in charge, putting things in order and closing doors. The medium said that he was unhappy we were in "his" area.

This information about the past administrator closing doors is interesting. For many months, from fall 2016 through early spring 2017, we found doors open that were previously closed when we arrived, as well as lights coming on in the locked offices of library staff. We had reports from staff and patrons that those offices had been targeted by spirits, with papers moved or thrown and books stacked where there weren't any when they had left the night before.

The spirits (perhaps those of past library staff and benefactors) seemed to keep tabs on the general goings on at the library. We had not been in the Webb for long one night when we heard through the P-SB11, near the circulation desk, "[Librarian's name], students, wrong." The previous night we had had to cancel an investigation due to a scheduling mix-up that involved a group of students using the library that night.

On Halloween 2017 there were several male spirits in the downstairs hallway and we heard, "Burnout" and "Yessir." Tonya saw a man in a dark blue wool suit in his thirties, possibly named Jacob, whom we may have previously encountered in early August facing the wall in the Cannon Room (see Chapter 16 for details).

Our guests were excited by the quick escalation of contact on Halloween night and were all taking flash pictures in the hallway. On the P-SB11 a spirit said, "Too much!"

In the chapter on the Children's Room you will read about a spirit we often interacted with named Michael. In the early months of the tour, we encountered Michael elsewhere on the first floor. One night he made a temperature gun decrease 12 degrees. Tonya heard his name and a sensitive with us that night asked if it was "Michael Reilly." On the P-SB11 we heard, "Yes/Yeah." We do not know if this was a different Michael or if "our" Michael was having some fun, as he sometimes did (he never responded affirmatively to the name Reilly after that night). Another night, while hearing "Michael" on the P-SB11 in the south end of the downstairs hallway, Tonya felt her arm pulled. She sensed it was the spirit of a little boy to whom Michael was attached in the Children's Room.

One evening in the south end of the first floor hallway we had a sustained conversation with a friendly spirit named Billy from the 1920s. Although he answered questions over the course of several minutes we never encountered him again.

On another night, there was movement at the end of the south end of the hallway by the Evans Street entrance and the EMF meters were going to orange. Guests saw something moving in the hallway at the north end as well. This happened again a week later, when a guest saw light moving in the first floor hallway near the Evans Street entrance. The EMF meters again went to orange. Tonya had previously seen two women and several other spirits through the Evans Street window in that area of the hallway.

Like Billy, many of the spirits we met at the Webb were transient. We only communicated with them for a single evening, or sometimes for a number of days or a few weeks. A good example of a spirit who was there for the first several months of our investigation is Josh. He was a big man in overalls, with a clear Southern drawl, who liked to answer in single syllables, "Yup" and "Yass" and the like (see Chapter 9 for how we met him). He showed up every night without fail. He moved freely around the first floor. We think he was a little envious of the attention that Dr. Thompson received, because he would at times pretend to be Dr. Thompson when we asked for the latter. The Southern drawl always gave him away.

Perhaps he moved on, or stopped making himself known, when Dr. Thompson continued to receive so much attention.

In the southwest corner of the first floor, at the entrance to what we called the Back Stacks (see Chapter 9), a guest who was sensitive felt like she was being forcibly stopped from entering. When we entered the stacks, Joey asked, "Is there anything you want to tell us?" The reply from the P-SB11 was, "Personal." The spirit box jammed. It began functioning normally when we left the area. We heard, "That is not cool" and again the spirit box jammed. Joey had switched to our second P-SB11 earlier in the evening because our primary spirit box had been jammed near the staircase.

See the section on the men's room in Chapter 8 for information on a spirit who often jams the P-SB11.

Not all the adult spirits in the Webb are authoritarian, angry, or jealous. In the next chapter, you will meet a man who was kind, wise, and communicated with us from the first time we entered the library right up through the completion of this book. His name is Dr. Thompson.

7
Take Your Medication
Dr. Thompson's Room

Dr. Thompson's ties to the land and building are the strongest of any spirit we encountered at the Webb, as evidenced by the volume and specificity of communications we received from him during our two-year investigation. As mentioned in Chapter 3, Dr. Sanford Webb Thompson Jr. sold one of the two lots that the Webb sits on to Earle Webb Sr. The lot he sold is now the courtyard.

Dr. Thompson made himself known to us from our first night in the Webb, in May 2016, although we did not learn his name for several weeks. As Tonya made her way through the library gathering impressions, she encountered a well-dressed man in a suit leaning against the eastern wall of the room that we gave his name. Her field notes describe an "image of distinguished man in a suit, black hair, 40–50ish, smoking and smiling." She got the word "fishing." Tonya thought he was quite handsome and charming, and each time she described these attributes the EMF meter spiked to red. In homage to *The X-Files*, Tonya named him "The Smoking Man."

Joey and Jonathan, the owner of Port City Tour Company, began asking The Smoking Man questions, responses to which came through the P-SB11:

Jonathan: Do you like to smoke?
The Smoking Man: Yep.
Joey: Cigars or pipes?
The Smoking Man: Both.
Jonathan: Anything else you'd like to say?
The Smoking Man: Fishing.

Of all the spirits in the Webb, he is the one most easily sensed by our guests. One night a medium sensed a man in Dr. T's typical area by the former fireplace. He said, "Hi" right after on the P-SB11.

Dr. Thompson's favorite place to stand.

During an investigation a week later, two teenage girls indicated that they were quite sensitive, and one of them described The Smoking Man to Tonya exactly the way she saw him. They also saw Oliver, the spirit boy in a news cap whom we encountered throughout the first floor. We did not yet understand their close relationship.

We received a clear communication through the P-SB11 that night. When we asked what The Smoking Man was smoking that evening, we heard, "Pipe." The following night, communications were faint and hard to make out, with the exception of a clear "Good evening" as we said goodbye to The Smoking Man before continuing our investigation in a different room.

It was an exciting moment several days later when Tonya called Joey from the local historical society. She had found the deeds for the Webb's two lots. One of the men who sold the property to Earle Webb Sr. was a doctor who had offices on the first floor. Now we had a name!

Several days later, we received confirmation from The Smoking Man that he was indeed Dr. Sanford Webb Thompson Jr., although, as we came to find out (through both research and communications with him), he liked to be called "Sam." These confirmations came through a combination of him nodding his head for Tonya as well as spiking the EMF meter to red. From that night, our interactions with Dr. T, as we affectionately called him, were more consistent and rich. Through ongoing research, we confirmed his age when he had offices at the Webb as Tonya saw him. He was born in 1888, so 40–50 was correct. He had his offices on the northern side of the building, where we communicated with him.

Dr. T's room was inviting to guests, who felt "pulled" there as we investigated the first floor hallway. Most guests, having never visited the library, had no way of knowing which room was his, yet the positive energy of the room—at least most nights—pulled them in, and the doctor was, more often than not, waiting to interact with them.

Before detailing those interactions, we want to share experiences we had with other spirits in Dr. T's room.

One night we heard a woman's voice come through the P-SB11. A medium with us sensed she was named Evie, Evelyn, or Emily. She asked the spirit if there was a birthday coming up and the woman said, "Yes." Tonya got the image of a cake.

We were unable to locate a floor map of how the doctors' offices were laid out on the first floor but based on the encounters we had and the energy of certain areas, we postulate that the Intro Room was an examining room and Dr. T's room was his office. That said, we did interact with a spirit in Dr. T's room for several weeks in July and August 2016 who was the victim of what our data suggested was a serious head trauma.

We first encountered this spirit, who did not know his name or where he was, in the Back Stacks. He appeared to mediums and communicated through the P-SB11 on several consecutive nights. We felt he was starting to trust us and get a better sense of who and where he was. After a week he was able to share with us that his name was Paul, and he knew he was in Morehead City.

In Dr. T's room on a night soon after, a guest sensitive saw Paul sitting in one of the chairs that flanked the magazine table. She felt as though Paul had been in an accident, and Tonya sensed that he suffered a head trauma, perhaps sustained while riding a motorcycle. He may have hit a telephone pole. There was a lot of anxiety on the first floor related to him that night, as expressed by numerous guests.

About a week later he said through the P-SB11 in Dr. T's room, "It's Paul." Joey asked if he was feeling better. Another spirit said, "No." We spoke to Paul several days later. He said his name and said, "It happened." A male guest about 15 years old who had an interest in the paranormal was holding the P-SB11 while sitting on a couch in Dr. T's room, which was a reliable spot for communication, when he felt head and neck pain and a tightening in his chest. The next night Paul said, "[indistinct] hospital." A week later, in Dr. T's room, a deep voice said, "Paul" and a woman's voice said, "Hospital." In the south end of the first floor, near the bookshelves where we initially met Paul, a sensitive asked about a head trauma a few nights later, and three days after that a paranormal investigator was strongly drawn to Paul's chair in Dr. T's room.

As we entered Dr. T's room, another male teen guest who was familiar with the P-SB11 sat on the couch near Dr. T's chair in the same spot the teenager had sat with the spirit box a few weeks before. Within moments he was complaining of high heart rate and left arm ache, which spread to his shoulder and neck. It was then that we realized he was not only the same age as our previous teen guest—he was holding the P-SB11 in the same spot on the couch and the two teens looked similar.

At that time, Joey asked if Paul was in the room. A female voice said, "Paul is wonderful," "Helping me," and "Never mind." Based on her tone of voice, Tonya felt the female was not being truthful in her communications.

Some days later a guest sitting on that same couch remarked that he felt twice his body weight. We did not receive a communication from Paul or any other spirit to explain what the guest was feeling.

Memorial Day weekend 2017, Tonya met a spirit who was showing her cards and money. We heard him say, "What's up?" on the P-SB11. When we asked his name he said, "Jerry" and "Hey—who's there?" Tonya shared everyone's names. Jerry showed that he was winning at cards. Tonya wished him luck and he said, "Bless you." Tonya described him as an African American between 20 and 30 years old and dressed in blue jeans and a white t-shirt. Jerry stayed with us the whole night and became a watcher/protector—at least, he tried to be (see the encounters with an interdimensional and with Men in Black in Chapters 13 and 16, respectively).

Jerry returned a few months later and said, "High dollar." Tonya pointed the EMF meter at the chair where he sat, and it spiked to red. We heard on the P-SB11, "Good choice" and "Great girls" (referring to our guests).

Not all the spirits we encountered in Dr. T's room were friendly. While we were communicating with Jerry the first time, another spirit manifested and pushed Jerry out of the way so he could talk instead, but Dr. T motioned to Tonya to shut off the P-SB11 to keep him from talking.

Another night a female voice on the P-SB11 said, "[unintelligible] this group." The tone was unkind. Joey asked if she wanted to talk to us. She replied, "No."

In August 2016 two sensitives sensed a spirit who did not want us in Dr. T's room. A week later we opened the door to Dr. T's room (which was usually open) and heard, "Close." One night we heard, "Strange." We asked, "Who moved the bookshelf?" (meaning the one that was vibrating in the stacks before we went to Dr. T's room; detailed in the chapter about that area). We heard, "Me" and "Hello" two times.

For the rest of the chapter, we focus on Dr. T. One night we had two clairaudients with us. They immediately went to the area where Dr. T customarily stood. Others in the group smelled his cherry pipe tobacco. We asked him if that was what he was smoking, and he responded, "Sure." The smell of the tobacco came and went throughout the first floor as we investigated.

Dr. T was by no means "trapped" or confined to "his" room. We encountered him throughout the first floor and even outside the Webb, which we detail at the end of this chapter and elsewhere in the book. He was sometimes gone or silent for considerable periods of time, such as much of July and early August 2016. This was a period of peak attendance for the investigation, with groups of 15–20 several nights a week. Dr. T was always more likely to communicate when the group was eight or less.

In the middle of August 2016 we heard, "He's here" and "Door" through the P-SB11. The EMF meter spiked red in his area but Tonya could not see him. A few days later he was there but didn't say much. A few guests smelled cherry pipe tobacco. Two days later he said he was "having a smoke." Tonya saw him reading a newspaper. At the end of September, a guest who smelled tobacco went over and stood in his spot by the fireplace and asked if a spirit smoked. Tonya told the guest that Dr. T did smoke, usually a pipe, and that he loved to fish. The guest told a story about a friend who threw back a large flounder earlier in the day. Dr. T shook his head in disbelief. One of the guests asked Dr. T if he could get a checkup. Dr. T laughed and shook his head no and mimed writing on a prescription pad.

Dr. T's primary mode of communication was miming or showing images of things to Tonya, like playing charades. Usually what he showed her was clear; on some occasions she could not figure it out, or it took a brief question-and-answer session.

One night, Dr. T was sitting in a newly placed chair in his space by the former fireplace. He allowed the two guests with us that night, a man and a woman, to sit in the chair. As the guests were taking pictures of each other in the chair, the facial recognition software on their phone focused on the area just above and behind the chair, at Dr. T's height.

He pointed to the man's head and showed Tonya a fedora. The guest had brought one on his vacation but had forgotten to wear it to the Webb. It was cold and Dr. T was concerned for the guest's health. He then played a violin for the woman and showed her white flowers. She asked if they were lilacs and if it might mean she would die. We were surprised by this question until she explained that she had been waiting for three years for a liver transplant. Ten and a half months later, this same couple was on their way to the Webb for an investigation. As they were driving she received a phone call—there was a probable donor for her long-awaited new liver at Duke Medical Center!

Almost a year later to the day of their visit to the Webb, Dr. T again showed white flowers to a guest. This time, they were lilies—the favorite flower of the guest and her daughter. He showed another guest a wedding veil. Her daughter had just gotten married and the guest's wedding anniversary was four days away. He lit his pipe and said, "Smell" while wafting his hand. We could!

Dr. T sometimes surprised us. One night he was dressed in a US Navy uniform with a commander's insignia. He kept saluting a teenage boy. We were unable to make a connection as to why this was happening. He had saluted guests before, including a Vietnam veteran, but we found no evidence he served in the military.

Dr. T served as a protector of the child spirits who inhabit the Webb and those who passed through. One night we encountered a spirit in the Back Stacks named Melissa. She could communicate using the EMF meter (Yes was red, No was green), and the P-SB11 temperature gauge rose and beeped in conjunction with her Yes responses. She was looking for her blond seven-year-old son, Adam. In Dr. T's room we heard a female on the P-SB11 say, "My children." Dr. T, miming to Tonya, directed us back to the Intro Room. Joey got goose bumps as we entered—a good indication of spirit activity. The male voice of a child on the P-SB11 said, "Mother." We asked if anyone else was in the room besides Adam and received no reply. After Tonya said she sensed that he was waiting for his mom we heard on the P-SB11, "Pick up." Tonya said that Dr. T was indicating to her that Melissa was upstairs. We went to what we call the Meeting Room. We heard a male's friendly laugh. When we went back downstairs Adam was by the Evans Street window in the Back Stacks. He said, "Mother." We did not encounter Melissa or Adam when we returned to the Webb a few nights later, or any time after.

On a different evening we heard a little boy's voice on the P-SB11, although what he was saying was unintelligible. Tonya saw that he was being drawn to a flower sitting on a magazine on the table. Tonya asked if he was the little boy named Adam who had lost his mother. He nodded yes. He crossed the room and sat on Dr. T's lap.

In addition to the investigations, we were involved with an educational program at the Webb for Port City Tour Company. Every spring, over numerous nights, nearly a thousand students learn about being a pirate. In 2017 we were brought in to offer a healthy dose of paranormal and ghost material. Before the program one night, Tonya was taking pictures of Dr. T's room. Each time she brought her camera up, the lamp next to her flickered. This happened several times. (During another presentation of this program in late April 2018—one day shy of the exact date in 2017—the lamp flickered on and off as Tonya told the students about Dr. T.) She also saw orbs through the viewfinder. The facial recognition software activated at a child's height and man's height, just like with our guest investigators in early December 2016. A few weeks later, before the educational program, the spirit of a little boy sat in Tonya's lap.

A week later, Joey had a custom-made animal mask on his table in Dr. T's room during his program on maritime superstitions and the supernatural at sea. As he talked, he and at least seven other people saw the mask rotate 15 degrees. The students who saw it lifted the mask and the tablecloth looking for wires—that's how sure they were that it moved.

The next night's educational program produced an interesting synchronicity: Tonya was telling a group of 30 students and their chaperones about Dr. T and she pointed to his chair. Everyone vocalized surprise: the boy who was sitting in the chair was also a Thompson!

A week later, Joey brought the animal mask back with him during an investigation to try and replicate some of the conditions of the previous week, to see if it would move. Although it did not, the EMF spiked to red near it, and Tonya saw Dr. T pointing to the little boy who has been with him recently, who was touching the nose of the mask. The librarian/authority figure that a medium saw in the first floor hallway the week before was watching from the opposite corner.

Oliver also liked to spend time in Dr. T's room. There were times when Tonya saw him in Dr. T's lap. One particular night, we had a temperature drop of five degrees under the table by Dr. T's chair. Oliver was sitting there. We got red on the EMF meters in the center of the couch as well.

One night in mid-August 2017 the spirit of a three-year-old boy named Nicholas was sitting on a couch in Dr. T's room. He wore a suit and had neatly combed hair. He held out his hand when a teenage girl who could see the vague shapes of some of the spirits that night sat beside him. When he took her hand, she felt a tingling sensation.

In February 2018 we met another little boy, perhaps seven years old, in suspenders. As he sat on one of the couches we heard the vinyl cushion compress! He got up from the couch after a few moments and touched one of the EMF meters. As he did, it spiked red. He moved behind one of the guests. She felt him pushing the back of her shirt. This was interesting because, a few minutes earlier, Dr. T was motioning to Tonya that we should go to the Children's Room across the hall. That is where the little boy wanted to go as well. We happily obliged.

The Wit and Wisdom of Dr. Thompson

After about a year of our interacting with Dr. T., he adopted a steady practice of choosing one of our guests (often someone sitting on the couch near his spot) to dispense some wisdom and advice to, be it medical or the general life variety (it's no wonder—his grandfather and father were doctors, as was his son). This wisdom and advice was not in response to specific questions asked of him by the guests or us. Tonya would ask, "Do you have any advice or messages for anyone in the room, Dr. T?" and he would then respond as he wished. The following list is from our field notes:

- Tonya was sitting in Dr. T's room. All day she had been experiencing blurred vision in her right eye. She asked Dr. T to look at it for her. He showed her two Advil and said she had an "enflamed ocular nerve" and this would help. She asked for confirmation that it was two Advil and the table lamp flickered and Dr. T nodded yes. His "prescription" worked! He must have enjoyed playing on the old trope of "Take two _____ and call me in the morning!" [Synchronicity: Exactly a year to the day later, Joey called Tonya with a question about this chapter. She was in a drugstore an hour away getting drops for blurred vision in her right eye.]

- Dr. T showed Tonya that a teenage guest in the group liked to play cards.

- Dr. T "diagnosed" one guest as dehydrated. She confirmed that she was hot and sunburned. The temperature in the area where she stood dropped several degrees (from 78 degrees in the room to 72.3 degrees where she stood). We felt that was Dr. T's way of offering her some relief.

- One of the female guests complained she had a scratch on her ear and thought a spirit might have done it. Dr. T said she scratched it with her nail.

- Dr. T motioned to our teen guests and made driving motions. One guest was driving his golf cart too fast the previous night and had been stopped and warned about it. The guest asked Dr. T how he knew. Tonya said it was because spirits have an expanded consciousness. Joey added that the memory was probably in the forefront of the teen's mind and the EMF spiked red in response.

- Dr. T motioned to a teen girl's hair. We asked if she had had it cut recently. She said, "Yes." He showed Tonya an image of the girl in a prom dress. She had been upset with her mother the night of her prom because her hair did not look like she wanted it to. Through miming to Tonya, Dr. T told the girl she had looked beautiful. The girl's mother showed us a photo of the girl the night of the prom. The dress was exactly like Tonya had described it. Tonya felt it was Dr. T's way of letting the girl's mother off the hook about the hairdo.

- Dr. T told a guest that her medical tests would turn out fine.

- Dr. T told a teen guest that he should not give up swimming. It was unclear if he meant as a competitor or as a coach. Dr. T showed him medals.

- He told a female guest that he liked the lemon-scented product she used in her hair.

- Dr. T acknowledged a teen girl who writes poetry in a journal. He encouraged her to keep doing that and literally applauded her.

- One night, Dr. T had a message that Tonya thought it best not to deliver in front of everyone. He indicated that a teenage boy in the group was drinking too much. It is our hope that Dr. T was able to plant a seed in the boy's mind of what he was observing.

- He told Joey to take a decongestant. Joey was having trouble with his ears due to allergies. Two nights later he wagged his finger at Joey because he did not follow doctor's orders. Joey took the decongestant the next day and his ears soon cleared up.

- He pointed to a guest and showed Tonya an image of her wearing a sundress. He showed her flowers. The guest did not know what it meant. Later that night, however, the guest sent a photo to our Facebook page of a ghostly image she had captured. Her Facebook profile picture was of her wearing a sundress with flowers on it.

- He indicated to one guest that she had been moving boxes that were too heavy and that was how she had injured her back. The guest confirmed that her family recently had to do a hurry-up move and that she had overdone it and injured herself.

- He pointed to a guest's daughter and indicated driving and her being upset and in fear. He said she did not need to be afraid. We learned she had recently been in a car accident.

- We had a guest who was an entomologist with us one night. Dr. T showed him a moth. As Tonya was asking for more details, a medium that Tonya was training was rapidly drawing what he was seeing. When the guest saw the drawing, he said it was a luna moth, which is native to Gainesville, Florida, where he was from. Using Tonya as an intermediary, Dr. T also described either a centipede or millipede to the entomologist.

- Tonya said one night that we all have psychic abilities and Dr. T said, "Right" on the P-SB11. On another evening Tonya said the same thing, to which Dr. T replied, "Yes."

- He told a guest, "Take your medication."

- One guest was having trouble with her wrist. She asked if she should put ice on it. Dr. T showed her how to wrap it.

- One night he acknowledged a fellow fisherman.

- He showed Tonya a red car, especially the gas tank and mirror. One of the guests with us was restoring one. The gas tank was the first item replaced and the car was missing its mirror.

- He acknowledged another guest's love of cooking and acknowledged her blond-haired son.

- Tonya asked Dr. T about our going upstairs one night in late August 2017, after we had been dealing for weeks with the angry spirits gathered there. He said on the P-SB11, "Oh boy" and "Watch out for the hallway." We had a difficult time with the spirits on the second floor that night.

- Halloween 2017: One of the guests, who had first participated in a Webb investigation six weeks earlier on a particularly active night, reported that she felt pain on her shin after feeling contact on her leg in the Back Stacks. We went to Dr. T's room to have a look. She showed the group a vertical line on her leg about two inches in length. As we watched, the line became a red spot that spread and appeared to all of us like a fresh burn. The guest, too, said the spot felt as though she had been scalded. She reported that she had awoken one night after visiting the Webb with scratch marks on her stomach, and her husband had been touched by an invisible entity.

Dr. T suggested that we ice the burn. One of the guests had ice and a clean bag in his car from a fishing trip earlier in the day—the same guest who had contacted us months earlier to request a special Halloween-night investigation. In an email weeks prior to visiting the Webb, this guest had also expressed interest in witnessing physical phenomena like scratches and bruises after hearing about those things from a guide on a local Ghost Walk a year earlier. The spirits in the Webb complied with his wish.

It took about five months for the mark to fade.

Epilogue

On January 6, 2017, Joey sat at his writing desk, editing a paper by a community college theater arts teacher so riddled with typos and badly constructed sentences that his frustration was high. His frustration became a verbal tirade when he read that this teacher was on a committee writing the National Standards for theater arts. The organization he worked for is one that Joey is a member of, has presented at conferences for, and has won playwriting awards from. As he expressed his frustration to Tonya, they simultaneously smelled cherry pipe tobacco. It filled the room. At first, we thought it was a neighbor, but the smell was too strong. It was as though the pipe was being smoked mere feet from us.

We knew it was a spirit. Joey's maternal grandfather used to smoke pipes with cherry tobacco and had always been a big supporter of his career in the theater, but that did not feel right. Joey said, "Maybe it is Dr. Thompson" just as Tonya saw him. Dr. T stood beside Joey and tapped his pipe on the computer screen where Joey was editing the paper. He showed Tonya that Joey should get in touch with the organization about becoming active in their programs again. Once the message was delivered, Dr. T and the smell of tobacco disappeared.

Synchronistically, Joey had received the organization's yearly journal in the mail the day before.

8
We'll Be in Touch

The Ladies' Room, Men's Room, and Basement

Along the first floor hallway were three rooms we did not consistently enter. Activity was rare in each, but when something did occur, it was notable.

The Ladies' Room

On our first trip to the Webb, Tonya saw a mournful woman in an early 1900s bridal gown next to the sink. When the bride saw Tonya, she ducked into a stall and out of sight. The next time we entered, she was at the sink again, unhappy to be seen.

When the investigations were opened to the public a week later, the ladies' room was one of the areas we visited. During one of our early investigations, the P-SB11's temperature gauge indicated the presence of a spirit. At the same time, an EMF meter registered in the mid-range (orange), and immediately after that, a handheld temperature gun indicated an eight-degree drop (from 81 to 73 degrees). Tonya asked, "Is our bride with us tonight?" Through the spirit box came a faint female voice, which sounded like a child, replying, "*I'm* here." Tonya asked if the bathroom was this spirit's favorite place, and from the spirit box came a clear "Yes" in a female voice that sounded much older than the first.

The next night we again sought out the bride. We had a similar temperature drop and EMF readings but did not receive any female communications. As we were leaving the room, we received a clear P-SB11 communication from a male, "We'll be in touch."

It was several months before we again encountered the bride. In November 2016 she tried to communicate on the P-SB11, but it was indistinct. In mid-February 2017 she was sitting on the couch near the old fireplace in Dr. T's room.

There were some physical phenomena in the ladies' room:

- The women's bathroom light spontaneously came on.

- The women's bathroom door opened while a teenage girl was in one of the stalls. Everyone else in the group was in a room well down the hall and all accounted for at the time.

- Before the guests arrived one night, Tonya took the opportunity to use the ladies' room. As she exited and the main door closed, we heard a stall door slam inside the bathroom. When the guests arrived, we tried to replicate the timing/sound and could not.

The Men's Room

In early July 2016 we investigated the men's room for the first time and inadvertently discovered and angered a spirit who was hiding in one of the stalls. Two clairaudients turned to each other within seconds of our entering and each spoke a version of the following, "I am hearing 'women do not belong in here.'" All the women left. Three men stayed behind. Joey asked if anyone wanted to talk. The reply was, "No." The P-SB11 malfunctioned, as if the frequencies were being jammed. We went into the hall and the spirit box resumed proper functioning. Joey tried our back-up P-SB11 in the men's room and the same thing happened.

For several weeks the male spirit jammed the P-SB11 in the first floor hallway and talked over other spirits trying to communicate. This testy male spirit never told us his name, although we asked several times. One night he was particularly agitated. At the one hour, 15-minute mark of the investigation (a time when many of the Webb's spirits were fatigued by our presence), he said, quite emphatically, "Bullshit." Another night he was more annoyed than usual. He stood by the stairs and jammed the P-SB11, which had a new battery. Outside of Dr. T's room he said, condescendingly, "Doc." Dr. T wasn't in his room that night; we suspected he was avoiding this spirit. In the hallway, the angry spirit said, "I'm here." As Joey approached the men's room door, the spirit said, "That's enough." Joey didn't enter.

A few nights later we had a temperature drop of five degrees and the EMF meters went to red in the men's room. People felt uncomfortable and had goose bumps. The P-SB11 jammed. Joey asked, "Are you there, sir?" and we heard, "No." On a night soon after that, he called us "dicks." He said some other things we could not make out but, judging by the tone, were equally unpleasant. Later in the evening, as we descended the stairs, he said, "Fuck you."

We also heard a deep male voice, indistinct, outside the Children's Room in mid-August that we believe was him.

In spring 2017, as our trouble with the angry male spirits upstairs started, Tonya sensed the aggressive male energy of the spirit from the men's room, although he did not communicate or interfere with the P-SB11.

In December 2017, for the first time in several months, we took a group into the men's room. We had a three-degree drop (66 to 63) on a temperature gun at the same time the temperature gauge went red on the P-SB11. Jolie saw a male face next to Joey's. She felt a tug on her sleeve at the elbow and a hand push her face. She felt he was trying to get away from us.

In early February 2018 Joey entered the men's room and asked if anyone was there. He got no response. Minutes later, in the hallway, everyone heard, "Going crazy" and "Damn fool" on the P-SB11 while the EMF meters were steady red. Joey had disturbed the male spirit and he was letting us know. A few weeks later Joey entered the men's room and immediately heard, "Screw you." He exited without delay.

You may be asking why Joey persisted in entering the men's room. The reason is we also encountered male spirits in the men's room who were friendly. One night Joey asked, "Is anyone in here?" From the P-SB11 we heard a teasing male voice say, "That's the question."

A different night, we heard, "What's up?" Although John from the Cannon Room used this phrase (see Chapter 16), it did not sound like him. Then again, John was not in the Cannon Room that night.

The Basement

When one thinks of a haunted house or building, the basement is one of the areas that creates the most interest and dread. Ironically, in the Webb, the basement was one of the quietest areas and one we rarely visited. It was small and cramped, with a low ceiling and low-hanging pipes and sections of the floor that were covered with water—not a place we wanted to take large groups of people for liability issues or navigation.

Around the time we started our investigations, Joey was having lunch with a local writers group. He was talking about a screenplay he was working on, a paranormal thriller, and one of the women at the table asked if he had ever been to the Webb. "As a matter of fact," he replied, "my wife and I have just been hired to lead investigations there." The woman said she was a former librarian and related that one day when she was in the basement alone she heard a growling in her ear.

The first few times we went into the basement, nothing happened. There were no readings on any of the temperature guns or EMF meters and no communication through the P-SB11. We decided there was no reason to go into the basement unless someone in a small group specifically requested it.

One night someone did. We received a single communication on the P-SB11 that said, "Chapter two." We took this to mean that the spirit was acknowledging that someone new had taken over the investigation. As you will see in later chapters, the spirits are well aware of who comes and goes, living or dead. Our emphasis on the stories of the Webb may have also provoked this response.

Months later, we were talking about the basement while standing in the first floor hallway—sharing what the librarian had heard and our one communication through the P-SB11. We ended by saying, "There is nothing much happening down there." At that moment, the deep voice of the angry men's room spirit replied, "Bullshit!"

On a night a few months later, Joey took a medium we were training, named Bryon, into the basement. Bryon heard a growl like the librarian Joey spoke with, which Joey had not previously mentioned to him. As that happened, through the P-SB11 came a deep male voice that said, "In the basement." The growl that Bryon described was almost identical to one Joey had heard in the Piano Room weeks before (see Chapter 15).

A few months later, we took into the basement a group of guests who had experience with paranormal investigation. We went to the end of the basement with them. Tonya felt a dark and malicious energy emanating from near the back wall. The energy felt so malevolent and sinister that she chose to wait until after the investigation to mention it to Joey. After a quick sweep with the equipment, we headed back to the first floor. Tonya had no further desire to explore the basement.

As we were finalizing this book, a former library volunteer invited us for coffee and told us that during an investigation several years ago a shadow being was witnessed in the basement.

Whatever growling entity lurks down there is better left alone.

The doors to the basement and ladies' room.

9
How Do You Do
The Back Stacks

The Back Stacks is what we called the area of the library on the south end of the building, facing Evans Street. It is a large area divided in two by the hallway, consisting of freestanding shelves, and some wingback chairs and small tables by the Evans Street windows. There is also a wingback chair with its back to Ninth Street. In early 2017 we started taking small groups there after the Intro Room to practice with the equipment. Prior to that, we began the investigation in the first floor hallway, but people were so excited and eager to have an experience they moved too fast. In the Back Stacks we had them move slowly and methodically, moving the EMF meters and temperature gauges carefully along the rows of books and around the furniture.

It was early in our investigation, in the heat and humidity of the 2016 Crystal Coast summer, that Tonya picked up the impression of a large male in overalls. Joey asked the spirit, "What do you see?" (a phrase suggested by a mentor) and a clear "You" came through the P-SB11, followed by the name "Josh" and "How do you do?"

Joey responded, "We're doing well. How are you?" The spirit answered, "I'm Josh." Joey asked, "Do you want to tell us anything, Josh?" He replied, "I don't want to talk," so we thanked him and said goodbye. He appeared again in the Back Stacks a few weeks later. As detailed in Chapter 6, Josh hung around the first floor hallway for several months.

In Chapter 7 we introduced you to Paul, the spirit who slowly regained his memory over time and repeated communications. It was in the Back Stacks in July 2016 that we first encountered him, confused and unsure of his name and where he was.

The spirits we encountered in the Back Stacks were overwhelmingly friendly. "Hello" is a communication we often heard on the P-SB11. One night a female spirit said, "Hello, Joe." Another evening a female spirit said, "We all ___ ___ party," "Hi," and "Hello."

Some weeks later we heard a male spirit say, "What's going on," "Hello, Joe," and "Artist," followed by piano music. As you will see when you read about the hip spirit named John in the chapter on the Cannon Room, this is typical of him. What makes this particular set of communications interesting is that we are almost certain John never appeared to us on the first floor, but the Cannon Room is directly overhead from where we received these communications in the Back Stacks.

A little boy said, "Hello" in the Back Stacks one night. We are not sure if it was Oliver, although he had been seen in the area. One night the boy was on his hands and knees. Tonya asked him what he was doing and he said, "Hiding."

As Joey walked past a chair by the window facing Ninth Street one night, he heard a male voice on the P-SB11 say, "Okay." A returning guest said that she and her boyfriend had arrived early and had seen someone in that window.

Communications in the Back Stacks were overwhelmingly female. In late August 2016 we heard female voices on the P-SB11 say, "Please go away" and "Hope we're next."

Another evening in August, a sensitive in the group said there was a woman named Elizabeth in one of the chairs. This was confirmation for Tonya, who had communicated with a Liz/Elizabeth from the 1920s a few times earlier in the summer. Elizabeth also said her name one night on the P-SB11. Elizabeth was in her chair in her white lace dress a few nights later, her hair in a bun. We heard a series of unintelligible older voices all around her on the P-SB11. She was also there the next night. In early September, there was a woman in a floral dress in the Ninth Street chair where Elizabeth usually sits, and then a woman in a house coat Tonya saw earlier in the summer. A few moments later a woman in a white dress from the early 1900s occupied one of the Evans Street chairs. Also, a woman moved with us through the stacks. She was dressed in more modern fashion than the spirits previously seen in that area.

This phenomenon of spirits gathering slowly in groups was not unusual in the Webb (especially at the south end of the building), as you will see in the chapters to come. Typically, an adventurous spirit would engage in communication and, due to our respect and gratitude, other spirits would steadily join us.

During late summer/early fall 2016 a man sat in the chair at the Ninth Street window on two different nights. Although he could be seen by Tonya and other sensitives, he did not verbally communicate, which was not surprising. Spirits often sat in the chairs or stood behind plants or other objects in the Back Stacks without communicating.

One evening, a female guest in the Back Stacks complained of arm and hand pain. Several of our guest investigators had reported being touched in the stacks on prior occasions, so we tried to make contact through the P-SB11. All we received is one communication, which sounded like "Barney."

On another night, an older woman wearing slippers sat in a chair with its back to Evans Street on the west side of the building. Tonya got the name "Glenda." She may have been a former resident at the nursing home or a patient in the hospital.

In December there was a strong smell of peppermint that Tonya and our two guests vocalized simultaneously. Joey felt it on his tongue but could not smell it.

Tonya saw a spirit sitting in one of the Evans Street chairs that she had seen months before standing outside the Webb in a seersucker suit (see Chapter 1), as well as a female standing elsewhere in the stacks.

One night, while investigating the west side of the stacks, we heard a deep male voice on the P-SB11 say, "Go away." We promptly headed upstairs. In that same area, about a week earlier, a guest got a burning sensation in the throat. Tonya had her elbow touched. A female voice on the P-SB11 said, "Especially don't." The peppermint smell from months before returned. Many months later we observed a young man sitting in one of the chairs in that area. Tonya asked his name and through the P-SB11 he said, "Don't ask me."

As we headed south down the first floor hallway toward the Back Stacks one night, a few of the guests saw movement, and the EMF meters registered orange. Guests also observed something moving in the hallway at the north end of the building. This happened a week later, when a guest witnessed light moving in the first floor hallway by the Back Stacks. The EMF meters again registered orange.

We received a plethora of random communications in the Back Stacks, including "Father," "Your father," and "For a minute." We also heard many names: Howard, Eric (we had a guest with that name the night we heard it), Stephanie, Brian, Dave/David, Daniel, and Dale. This fits hand in glove with the fact that the Portal Hallway (see Chapter 12) was above these rooms. It was usually filled with transient spirits and generated a great deal of random communication.

As we moved to the Back Stacks one night at the end of March 2017, almost everyone in the group felt a heavy energy. Tonya sensed a woman with a first name beginning with M. There was also a strong scent of sawdust on the west side of the stacks, but no evidence of recent construction and no sawdust anywhere around.

One afternoon in the summer of 2017 we received a text from a colleague saying her five-year-old son had seen a "man on fire" standing in front of the window on the western Evans Street side of the stacks facing the Bask Hotel (the former hospital and nursing home).

That night we found the "man on fire" outside the library by the window on Evans Street, near where the boy saw him. The EMF meters were spiking red and there were some photographic anomalies—blurred shadows and unexplainable shafts of light. We attempted to cross him over in a manner similar to the one we used in the "Portal Hallway" weeks earlier (see Chapter 12), but he was afraid and unsure about what was beyond the light.

Later that evening we returned to the window on Evans Street. The "man on fire" was still there. We tried again to cross him over. His presence according to the EMF meters was now weaker. Joey sent the thought, "Go into the light" and from the P-SB11 came, "I think."

The area in the Back Stacks where the "man on fire" was seen.

The "man on fire," whose name he finally told us was Robert, was brought to our home by one of Jolie's spirit guides, William, who was with us at the Webb that night. William is an Army veteran from World War II and may have been compelled to look after a brother in arms. According to a dream Jolie had, Robert was taken back to the Webb in the middle of the night by Dr. T and Oliver. Dr. T was unhappy that William had taken Robert to our house instead of leaving his care to the doctor. Tonya had seen Oliver in the Back Stacks looking at Robert during our investigation that night.

Robert was back at the Webb when we returned the next evening, still unwilling or unable to cross over. Two weeks later, he was no longer there.

One night a few months later a temperature gun increased 14 degrees (from 67 to 81) near the Evans Street chairs. An *increase* is extremely rare with the temperature guns. It was early fall and the heat was not on. We believe another burn victim from the hospital in that area was trying to communicate.

For several nights in the summer of 2017, at a time when the Webb's activity was at its height, one of the bookshelves in the Back Stacks was vibrating without explanation. Night after night guests felt it, first in their feet from the floor around the bookshelf and then by putting their hands on it. There was no machinery below it that explained the vibration. Additionally, the EMF meters were going to mid-range (orange) as it vibrated. One night a guest saw two spectral faces floating in front of the shelf.

In October 2017, Joey, in an instance of clairaudience, heard the name "Maria" in his head after a sensitive saw a woman's spirit and he asked if that was her name. She nodded and the EMF meters went to red.

We were unable to locate photos of the doctors' offices on the first floor. A doctor named Benjamin Franklin Royal, who was instrumental in the building of the Morehead Hospital and who ran the burn ward there during World War II, had offices where the Back Stacks are. Bryon, one of the mediums that occasionally worked with us, "saw" a desk with a person behind it on the east side of the Back Stacks. This might be evidence of Dr. Royal's offices.

Although we never encountered Dr. Royal in the Webb, he introduced himself to Tonya in early February 2018 while she was at the Bayview Cemetery in Morehead City, where we had learned Dr. T was buried. Bayview is large and does not have markers for way finding, so Tonya was having a hard time locating Dr. T's grave. She called upon his spirit to help her. Instead of Dr. T, she saw the spirit of a middle-aged man pointing to a section of the cemetery. Following the spirit's directions, she came upon the grave of Dr. Royal. Based on pictures we have of him, she confirmed that it was indeed the good doctor who wanted her to see where he is buried.

On Halloween night 2017 there was a woman whose name began with E sitting in one of the chairs on the west side of the Back Stacks. The spirit named Elizabeth sometimes sat there, but it was not she. The energy was strong enough that several guests and Joey each felt it in their solar plexuses. There was also a three-degree drop in temperature. The spirit said, "I was____" (embalmed? evolved?). She also said, "Russia."

Moving to the east side of the stacks, we encountered an athletically built spirit named Michael (a prevalent name in the Webb) sitting in a chair on the east side of the Back Stacks. Tonya had first seen him almost a year earlier. This time, he was dressed like a freight train conductor. He said, "Hello." Our guest investigators asked him questions. When one said, "Your train brought supplies to the ships," he said, "Exactly." (See Chapter 3 for the history of Morehead City's port and railroad.)

We watched as the creases in the back of the chair changed, as if someone was making an impression on it with their back and shifting position. We realized that a different spirit inhabited the chair. It was the father of one of our guests. (See Chapter 17, "Communications from Deceased Friends and Family," for details of this emotional reunion.)

Several months later, we again watched as the creases on the back and seat of that chair changed before our eyes. The EMF meters spiked red, the P-SB11 registered a temperature change increase (indicating a spirit was attempting to come through), and Tonya and a sensitive saw the spirit of an elderly gentleman standing up and sitting down. He could not communicate and appeared to be confused. Tonya asked everyone to envision white light and call upon angels to help him. The angels answered the call and led him into the light.

A few weeks prior, the spirit of another young man in his twenties was sitting in one of the other chairs in the area. He was dressed like a drum major, in white and gold. According to Tonya's research, parades, including marching bands, down Arendell Street (Highway 70) were popular in the 1940s and 1950s. We could not discern his name, although it began with an S. While we were trying to communicate with him, a temperature gun dropped five degrees. As we were leaving the Back Stacks, a male voice said, "Thank you."

We all said, "You're welcome."

10
This is the Fun Room
The Children's Room

In the twenty-first century, libraries around the United States are less of the community centers than they used to be. More and more adults (and children!) read on mobile devices. Checking out traditional books from the library has become a novelty with younger generations, leaving libraries to struggle for both patrons and funding.

An exception to this trend is the Webb. Every day, dozens of children and their parents fill its hallways and rooms. Many of these children have spoken about the spirits they see, and it is not unusual for them to ask their parents if they can take their "new friend" home with them—a friend few can see. Some even mention the spirits by name.

Like the children we heard about in our interviews with patrons and staff, we communicated with many spirits in the Children's Room at the Webb. Appropriately, we begin this chapter with the child spirits we met in our two years of investigation. As you will see, plenty of adult spirits were also in the Children's Room, and we believe they made themselves known as often as did the child spirits, based on the names we heard during our interviews.

Child Spirits

One of the most moving experiences that guests had during our investigations was with the spirits of children that reside in the Webb.

The Children's Room is filled with books, toys, stuffed animals, and games. We watched with delight each evening as our adult investigators traveled back in time to when they were children as they crossed the threshold of the room and fanned out toward its offerings.

The Children's Room.

Early in our investigation we heard a communication on the P-SB11 while Tonya saw two small children running around the bookcases: "Ah, this is the fun room!" It proved to be exactly that.

In late March 2017 a medium immediately sensed children playing hide-and-seek. This corroborated previous impressions received by Tonya as well as other guest investigators and mediums. That summer, guests sensed a little boy in the Children's Room named Steven. He made the temperature guns drop several degrees and the EMF meters spike to red on a lower shelf behind a wicker basket full of stuffed animals where he liked to play Hide and Seek. A sensitive had sensed him and two other children giggling and running around before they hid behind the basket.

The shelf behind the wicker basket often spiked red on the EMF meters. The child spirits loved to hide there. If the wicker basket was *not* in front of the shelf, we got no readings on the EMF meters. If we placed the wicker basket in front of the shelf and waited a few minutes, the EMF meters would spike to red. After all, you can't hide if there's nothing to hide behind!

As the guests played along with the hide-and-seek, Joey said that one of the little boy spirits "is wise to you guys" (this was a "knowing" he had: he could not see the little boy) and a female voice on the P-SB11 said, "Wiiiiiiise." We heard a spirit say, "Hey _____" (the name of a medium with us that night).

One evening in July 2017 two sensitives saw the spirit of a 12-year-old boy waving his arms and jumping up and down in a corner of the Children's Room as if to say, "Look at me!" He was later playing with a puzzle in a different corner. Two nights later he wanted to play checkers with a girl who was a sensitive. As she was setting up the checkers on the board, a man on the P-SB11 (possibly Michael, an adult spirit you will meet later in the chapter) thought she was going too slow and said, "If you live long enough." The boy said, "She's in the red" (she had chosen to play the red checkers). In mid-August the 12-year-old was back in the room. When Tonya saw him, a voice on the P-SB11 said, "Describe it," so she told the guests about how he liked to jump up and down and wave his arms.

A few weeks later, a man heard a little girl whisper in his ear. He asked if there was a little girl behind him. Tonya confirmed there was and that she wore a red and white dress (she saw this little girl about a year before) and she wanted something in his pocket. He had a piece of candy there! The man offered the candy to the spirit of the little girl by placing it on a table. As we were leaving the room, Tonya asked if he wanted to take the candy with him. He could not conceive of the idea. He was still unsettled by the little girl whispering in his ear and did not want to risk her tagging along with him. Ideally, we would retrieve the candy the next morning and dispose of it after the little girl had taken its essence, but we could not leave a piece of candy sitting on the table for the librarians to find the next morning, so we placed it carefully in a clean trash can that had been emptied at the end of the work day.

In early September 2017 the spirits of two boys were in the Children's Room. A guest asked if they liked to read. A few moments later the EMF meters lit up intermittently red by two boxes of books. Through trial and error, we found a Batman book that lit up the EMF to a steady red. As Joey pulled it from its box, we heard on the P-SB11, "Batman." One of the guests read some of the book and a guest medium said that one of the boys was jumping up and down and clapping his hands with delight. After the guest read several pages the adult spirit named Michael said, "All right" (as in, "That's enough reading."). The temperature guns dropped between six and nine degrees.

On Halloween night 2017 several guests sensed a spirit near the shelves at the back of the room. The EMF was going to red consistently while two guests played with the Duplo blocks that sat on a table in the center of the room. Tonya again saw the little girl in the red and white dress. Guests were also capturing images and video of orbs on their cell phones. Oliver was also present. Another sensitive felt her hair touched, which was something Tonya had felt when we first entered the room.

In February 2018 Joey was standing by a female guest near the checkerboard. She said she was being touched on the hand. Joey asked if it was a gentle touch and she replied yes. Tonya came over and saw the little girl touching her hand. At that moment the woman said the hairs on her neck stood up and she tingled from head to toe. The little girl stayed with her while we remained in the Children's Room. The woman's camera would not take a clear picture: a haze or mist covered all the photos. Her husband took pictures right next to her with no hazing at all.

A few weeks later, the spirit of the little boy in suspenders, whom we earlier mentioned had pushed on the woman's back to go into the Children's Room, was sending one of the EMF meters to solid red as he sat in a chair by a basket of crayons. Joey sat by the Duplo blocks and the spirit of a little girl sat in a chair next to him. Another EMF meter a guest held by the chair spiked red.

Moving Objects
Early in our investigation we heard on the P-SB11, "Books fly off shelves

in here!" and we got a strong sense that objects did indeed move around the room. As time went on, our intuition was backed up with experience.

One of the centers of activity early on was the wooden chess and checkerboard table at the back of the room. After the EMF meters spiked while we moved them over the small basket containing the chess pieces and checkers, we set up and photographed the chess pieces. When we returned 30 minutes later, it was clear that one of the pieces had moved.

After setting up the chess pieces on another night, an EMF meter spiked red when anyone touched the pieces. Again, upon returning to the room later, photographic evidence showed a piece had been moved.

A featherlike bookmark hung from one book's bottom. At least five people, including Joey, watched the feather move and sometimes slowly twist back and forth on different nights. There was no vent above or below the book and no other mundane explanation why the bookmark moved.

As we said earlier, the Children's Room has lots of stuffed toys and dolls. A pair of observant investigators noticed one night that one of the dolls—the Abby character from Sesame Street (who, appropriately enough, is a fairy)—had been moved when we returned to the room near the end of our investigation.

From that night on, we had a guest place Abby on the floor of the room and arrange her hair and hair ribbons in an easily discernible pattern and then had several guests photograph her. We returned about 4 minutes later, at the end of the night, and had the guests compare her with the photos while we stood well away. On several occasions there was a noticeable difference.

In February 2018 it looked like Abby was moved slightly by the spirit of a little girl who was fond of one of our guests, although the movement was hard to tell. When Tonya put Abby back where she belonged a cold spot developed around the woman, and Tonya realized the little girl was unhappy that Tonya had put Abby away. Tonya moved Abby to a child-sized rocking chair and the cold spot vanished. Joey had been busy making notes and had missed hearing that the doll moved. When he asked if that was the case, Tonya and the woman said, "Probably." Simultaneously, the word "probably" was heard from the P-SB11.

In July 2016 we left a small stuffed dog in place for 45 minutes and when we return to check on it we found that it had moved three inches and rotated 45 degrees.

The Abby doll. Notice the burst of light in the first photo and the change in the ribbon below her skirt in the second.

As we were getting ready to leave after checking the Abby doll one night in early fall 2016, Joey and two guests were standing by a six-inch-tall wooden bear figure on top of a shelf. It rocked back and forth in front of their eyes.

After the tour ended one night in mid-summer 2017, one of the guests, a skeptic looking for a paranormal experience, asked to stay on. He took Joey back to the Children's Room and showed him a mobile of a monkey. He said that it had been moving on its own when we were there earlier in the night. As we watched it, a panda mobile two feet away rotated. There were no air vents anywhere near either of them.

98

Michael

We have mentioned Michael twice in this chapter. It is time for you to meet him. He was one of the most talkative and engaging of any of the spirits in the Webb. He had appointed himself guardian of the Duplo blocks in the room. We first met him in early August 2016. Tonya could clearly see him, and his facial expressions and gestures matched what he said on the P-SB11, which was quite a lot.

Our relationship with Michael began when Joey could not resist sitting at the table with the Duplo blocks and building something as the guest investigators fanned out in the room, using the equipment to look for activity. As Joey was building, we heard agitated but unintelligible communication coming from the P-SB11. Tonya said that it was a man sitting on the couch right by the Duplo table and that he was unhappy Joey was playing with the blocks. He was not so much angry as feeling "adults should not be playing with these."

This pattern played out over and over through the summer and fall of 2016. Joey sat at the table and Michael communicated. Sometimes other guests—all females—asked if they could build something with the blocks. Inevitably, as they started to build, Michael called them names. Once he did, we put the blocks away. One of the females was a radio DJ who came with her team one night as a special promotion.

Joey was setting up the Duplo blocks another night, and Michael got unusually agitated. He said, "Don't touch it." When Joey stopped, he said, "Better." A female guest started playing with them and he called her a "bitch." Another night a teenage male was playing with the blocks, which was fine with Michael. The teenager's mother started playing with them and from the P-SB11 came "Stop."

A few nights later, as Joey set up the blocks, Michael asked, "What are you, a child?" The next night he was agitated when a guest reached out to touch them, yelling "No!" and "Stop!" We made sure no one touched the blocks the rest of the night. Two days later, a sensitive, upon witnessing Michael's response to Joey playing with the blocks, said Michael made a show of getting upset because it affected Joey. A paranormal investigator who also joined us that night was kind to Michael, asking permission to touch the blocks, which made him happy.

When we entered the room one evening, all the blocks were stacked up. Michael was motioning for Joey to put them away. About halfway through his doing so Michael said on the P-SB11, "Too slow, man." A few nights later he said, "Hi," and when Tonya remarked to the guests that it was Michael, he said, "Apparently." He later said his name.

On a different night, Joey started putting away the stacked blocks that were on the table when we entered the room, thinking that was what Michael wanted. Instead, Michael got upset. He said, "Stop." Joey asked if Michael had put the blocks on the platform and Michael replied, "Some." Joey asked who else had put them on and he said, "Just me." Tonya had been theorizing that perhaps Michael was related to one of the male child spirits that frequented the room. She asked him if he was waiting for his son and he said, "No."

Joey sat down in front of the blocks a few weeks later and before he even touched them, Michael said, "Don't. Watch it. Don't." A teenage male started using the blocks. Tonya said that Michael was okay with the boy using them. When the teenager was finished with them, he asked, "What should we do with the blocks?" and Michael replied, "Put them away. Put them in the box."

Michael, as you can see, was quite human in his range of emotions and moods. One night he was happy and said it was okay for everyone to play with the blocks. "Just don't break 'em," he said. He asked that we "put the truck on the board" (a Duplo truck that is included with the set, which was sitting in the bucket of blocks), and he stated he didn't want a big green piece that Joey lifted out of the box of blocks on the table. Another night, Michael was calm. His mood was neutral. But he did say, "Stop" when two of the guests started using the blocks.

As a guest was building with the Duplo blocks in the spring of 2017, we heard from the P-SB11, "Here he is." Tonya said that one of the little boy spirits had come into the room and was showing the guest certain blocks he wanted him to use. As Tonya told the guest which blocks, the guest happily complied.

Michael was more active than usual one night in mid-July 2017. Through the P-SB11 he said, "Very well," "Put away the blocks," and then "Directions" in response to what Joey should build with them. He then said, "People," as though he were annoyed with us. The P-SB11 jammed. The light went blue on the temperature gauge, indicating that a spirit was angry. When the spirit box was reset Michael said, "Hello" as though he had calmed down and all was forgiven. Another night he expressed interest in one of the temperature guns. Perhaps it was the laser light feature that fascinated him.

In early August Joey and another male guest used all the Duplo blocks to build a castle. Michael said, "Hello" as they started. When they asked what he thought after they were finished, he said, "Okay" without much enthusiasm.

On Halloween 2017 Michael communicated a great deal through use of an EMF meter. He was able to let the guests know if he liked what they were building by making it spike red. He indicated to a pregnant guest that she was going to have twins in the same way (we never received confirmation on whether he was correct).

In early February 2018 we were in the midst of an active night and Joey didn't have the opportunity to use the Duplo blocks. As we were getting ready to move on, Tonya said Michael was showing displeasure that Joey had ignored the blocks. Joey made some time, with the help of a guest, to build a quick building. As they fit the blocks together, two excited voices were heard on the P-SB11. One was Michael and the other was Oliver. Later in the evening, when we returned to the room to check on the Abby doll (which had moved), Joey put away the blocks. As usual, Michael indicated he was being too slow about it.

Other Adult Spirits
In June 2016 we heard an unintelligible woman's voice come through the P-SB11. When we indicated we could not understand her, a clear "Come on people!" was heard by all the guests. Tonya politely apologized, stating that we sometimes had difficulty understanding what came through, to which the voice replied, "Excuse me?" She was clearly unsympathetic about our difficulties.

About a month later we met a spirit named Caleb, who engaged us in the longest exchange we ever had with a spirit on the P-SB11. First, he told us his name. We asked his age and he had some fun with us, saying, "Seven. Eleven." The conversation went on for about six more exchanges. Although Caleb wasn't around during our next visit, an adult female voice took up the game and said that she was "seven."

On an active night, with spirits of children running around and Michael expressing his feelings about our using the Duplo blocks, Tonya saw a spirit of a man who stood up from behind the couch where

Michael sits. As she saw him, and vocalized to the group what she saw, he said through the P-SB11, "Oh God!" as his eyes went wide in surprise that Tonya could see him! He quickly got used to us and played peek-a-boo from behind the couch with the guests. A month later he was back behind the couch and said, "Hi." One night a few weeks later he was making sounds by the bookshelf behind him that several people heard. A guest sensed someone in the back of or sitting on the couch.

In February 2018 we learned his name. One of our guests noticed the name "Hugh" spelled out with magnetic alphabet letters. When he asked if the spirit's name was Hugh, Tonya reported that the spirit's eyes got wide and he puckered his lips in surprise that we figured it out. She repeated his name and he again puckered his lips.

We had several synchronicities happen in the Children's Room. One night the name "Julian" came through the P-SB11. This happened to be the name of a sensitive's son.

There was a *Clifford the Red Dog* book on the couch one night. A guest named Clifford said that his aunt read it to him all the time as a kid. He said her husband was Frank. Tonya heard that name said in her mind just before the guest said it.

Aside from Michael's occasional bad moods, we did not have much experience with angry spirits in the Children's Room. One evening, several guests heard from the P-SB11, "Leave." Tonya asked, "Who is this?" and a voice on the P-SB11 repeated her words back to her. A few weeks later, there was an indistinct voice in the room. Joey asked, "Who is this?" A voice on the P-SB11 answered, "Somebody." Joey: "Michael, is this you?" The P-SB11: "Not me." A deep male voice said, "No need to [unintelligible]" and a female voice said, "How [unintelligible]er." Another night we heard, "You're out of time." On the night that the little girl was so excited about the Duplo blocks, a male voice on the P-SB11 that wasn't Michael said, "No!"

A few minutes later, Tonya said, "Let's go upstairs." The male voice said, "Bad idea." One of the guests said, "I want to go up there." The voice replied, "No. Don't." Another guest asked the little girl if she wanted to come upstairs. The little girl replied, "Noooo!" in a scared voice. (The guest did not know that the upstairs is not a place for child spirits.) The little girl stayed behind.

102

Tonya tried to communicate with Oliver one night in the Children's Room after he had visited her at her massage studio, which was 15 minutes from the Webb. She said, "I liked when you visited me in my studio." An adult male voice on the P-SB11 said, "He doesn't." Tonya replied, "Not any more" and the male voice answered, "Fine."

We heard banging coming from the Children's Room one night while we were coming down the stairs. A female voice on the P-SB11 said, "The world [unintelligible]" and "Just don't." We asked how many people were in the room and she said, "Twenty-five." We then heard a male voice say, "Buddy!"

In the back of the Children's Room one night we heard what we think was the spirit of a former librarian, who was often heard in the main entrance area, ask brusquely, "What is this radar?" most likely referring to the P-SB11.

With large groups, things could get chaotic in the Children's Room, with so much communication and data coming in on the equipment. One evening a male voice was coming through the P-SB11 but we could not understand him. Half the guests were investigating the other side of the room and were talking excitedly. The male spirit said, "Talking!" in frustration.

One night a guest asked where the chalk was in the Children's Room. The responses on the P-SB11 were "Chalk," "Keep up," and "Yeah." Another night we heard a friendly "Here we go" and "Hello."

One evening in late summer 2016 we had a group of more than 20, many of whom were cynics who had joined the investigation to debunk it. A few of them snuck away at some point and moved many of the stuffed animals and dolls around the room, as well as the chess and checker pieces. A week later we were sharing with a few guests that someone had tried to prank us and from the P-SB11 we heard, "Scruples."

As we said in previous chapters, the spirits at the Webb knew who came and went. In December 2017, Jolie was our medium for an investigation while Tonya recovered from surgery. As we entered the Children's Room a concerned male voice said "Tonya" on the P-SB11, acknowledging her absence.

Before we close this chapter, we want to address a concern that some of our guests had about the fact that spirits of children remain in the Webb for long periods of time. One of our teenage guests expressed that she was sad about it. This is understandable, given what films, TV, and novels tell us about "trapped" spirits and the necessity of crossing spirits into the light. But the children in the Webb, with few exceptions, were happy. As you can see from the stories in this chapter, they were playful, and the adults around them, such as Dr. T and Michael, look after them. They are in a place they clearly love, that is filled with toys, books, and the daily presence of other children. It is our feeling that these children are exactly where they want to be.

11
There's Just the One
The Staircase and Central Part of the Upstairs Hallway

The staircase in the Webb is more than just a means of getting from the first floor to the second—it signifies a noticeable vibrational shift between the floors. The feeling most mediums and sensitives got on the stairs and at the top landing was different from the sense they got on the first floor, where the occupants were like a "family" of residents who had clearly defined roles within the space. Even keeping in mind that hot air rises and, especially in the summer, the second floor was much warmer and the air "heavier" due to coastal humidity, there was a palpable and sharp activation of the body's warning systems when we climbed the stairs about midway through a typical night's investigation.

We encountered several spirits and anomalies on the stairs.

Halfway up the staircase one night, several members of the investigation experienced physical discomfort and a feeling of unease. These sensations were so strong that a few returned to the first floor to wait for the rest of the group.

In July 2016 a father brought his three daughters to the Webb. The youngest daughter, 12, did not feel comfortable touring the building, so Tonya kept her company in the Intro Room while Joey conducted the investigation with the man and his two older daughters. When they got to the top of the stairs, Joey and the others distinctly heard on the P-SB11, "There's just the one," as if one spirit was saying to another (or several) that Tonya and Joey were not together.

As Joey told the guests one night it was time to go upstairs, a voice from the P-SB11 said, "Wait." The P-SB11 went dead. As we paused to honor the request, Joey opened the battery compartment and one of the contacts of the nine-volt battery was detached. He always keeps the contacts tight, so it was "pulled off." At the same time, a medium sensed an elephant. As we headed up the stairs, the mystery was solved—there was an elephant planter on the landing. Later, when Joey told Tonya about the nine-volt battery being detached, a voice on the P-SB11 said, "Yeah."

One night in the summer of 2017 we had what can only be called a *confrontation* with the angry male spirits inhabiting the kitchen area upstairs. We relate the details of that encounter in Chapter 13, "The North Hallway and Kitchen," in order to keep the context and integrity of the overall experience with these spirits unified.

When we reached the top of the staircase each night, we took the opportunity to have guests take photographs and adjust to the more oppressive atmosphere of the second floor while we pointed out the unique architecture, which consists of two hallways—one with entrances into rooms on either side and the other with no entrances at all. See Chapter 18 for our theories as to why this architecture is a key reason why the Webb is so haunted.

Considerable physical sensations were reported on the second floor landing, including the sensation of being hot or having a fever, feeling flushed in the face, and shaking or aching legs. As the investigation was winding down upstairs one evening in early summer 2016, six people reported a heavy feeling that was greater than what guests usually felt when reaching the top of the stairs. At the same time, the six people simultaneously felt a tightness in their throat, as if someone was gripping it, similar to what Joey felt in the area behind the kitchen in our first investigation of the Webb (see Chapter 13 for the story of Joey's experience and the complete story of the spirit responsible, whose name is Vincent); at that point, we ended our investigation of the upstairs, foregoing our return to the Children's Room and the Intro Room as well.

We had to make a similar decision several nights later. As we climbed the stairs the energy was unusually calm. We thought Vincent was at last calming down. We were wrong. After almost 15 minutes, the group noticed the familiar heated energy and oppression we had come to expect. Joey realized that Vincent was not becoming used to us or calming down—he had simply been more patient. The feeling was so overwhelming that, with the agreement of the guests, we wrapped up our investigation of the upstairs and bid goodnight to the Webb and its occupants as quickly as we could.

For several nights after, as we made our way to the second floor, we received, through the spirit box, the same insults and displays of anger we had come to expect from Vincent, who did not enjoy visitors. Another spirit, perhaps attempting to warn us he was around, said, "Vincent" on the P-SB11 one night.

Variations on this theme unfolded for months, although never as severe as what we just described. One night in late summer 2016 our investigation of the second floor was at first quiet; however, after 20 minutes, Vincent made it clear that we had overstayed our welcome. We took a minute to share with our shaken guests some of our experiences with Vincent and expressed that he seemed to get impatient when we stayed upstairs longer than 20 minutes. By this time everyone was noticing the familiar, uncomfortable feelings associated with Vincent, so we decided to head downstairs. When one of the teenage girls in the group expressed that she felt bad that we stayed too long, Joey joked, "He'll get right over it," at which point, from a digital recorder that was *turned off,* a male voice echoed, "Get over it!"

Descending the stairs on a different night, Joey felt himself pushed forward by unseen hands. He had to plant his feet and throw his weight back to keep from tumbling down the stairs.

One night in March 2017, as we finished the investigation upstairs, we heard a voice through the P-SB11 say, "Leave right now." As we headed downstairs, Joey told the guests that this was not an unusual request. The spirits seemed to have had enough after about 90 minutes of our touring the Webb. While Joey was talking, we received one last communication from the P-SB11, "Really. Leave." As we always did when the request was that forceful, we did.

107

At the top of the stairs about a month after, we heard a female voice say, "I'm the same," and the P-SB11 jammed. Joey's flashlight blinked on and off (it was not the batteries; many weeks later, the same batteries were still in the flashlight and it was working fine).

At the top of the stairs was a distinct cold spot. This was rare; as we have said, usually it is warmer upstairs. And the cold spot was only in a less than three-foot-square area. We experienced other physical anomalies at the top of the stairs as well. Not only had the hallway lights been inexplicably turned on, the light in a locked second floor office had also come on. Once, as we reached the top of the stairs, three of us saw a light in a different locked room switch on. This happened a few more times in subsequent months.

One evening Joey was standing in front of one of the locked offices when he felt a presence behind him. At that moment, Tonya saw something move behind him. In that area almost a year later, Tonya saw the figure of a man standing there.

Some of the spirits we encountered on the stairs and landing liked having fun with us. During one of our last investigations, Joey told the guests we were going downstairs and a voice on the P-SB11 said, "Go downstairs." When we were halfway down, it said, "Going down the stairs." During another investigation, Joey was at the top of the stairs with the P-SB11 when a voice said, "Someone's dead." Tonya received an impression of the name "Sally" and we asked if there was a Sally present. After several moments a male voice came through and replied, "I'm Sally."

On Halloween night 2017, several things of note occurred. We were excited by the opportunity to have the husband of one of our guests set up and monitor four 360-degree cameras throughout the two floors. As often happened when cameras were set up in the second floor hallway, the camera did not work for the first part of the evening. After a great deal of examination of the video footage later by the guests, it was reported to us that they saw odd shadows and orbs.

As we headed up the stairs we heard a male voice say, "Go" on the P-SB11 and the whole group heard two howls *without benefit of the spirit box* at the end of the hallway opposite the kitchen as we reached the top of the stairs.

As Joey was talking about the architecture of the second floor, one of the guests who was a sensitive with training in shamanism shrieked and ran toward Joey, grabbing his arm in fright. She described a five-foot-tall, grey, wraithlike figure that had charged toward her from the north end of the hallway. The P-SB11 jammed soon after and when it came back on there was a prolonged radio voice talking about Halloween. This was the first time we had ever picked up radio for more than a split second (the antenna was down and the radio function was off). The battery was completely drained. As Joey was changing the battery, a female voice was heard by several guests in an instance of group clairaudience.

Soon after, the group heard another howl, followed by a growl.

As you will see in the chapters that follow, these kinds of phenomena only got more intense as we went down the halls and into the rooms of the second floor.

12
It's a Portal
The South Hallway

The changes in energy that we experienced on the second floor almost certainly emanated from—and were compounded by—the 25 or so feet of mystery that is the south hallway. With a window at the end (facing the Bask Hotel) but no entranceways into any of the second floor rooms (unlike the north hallway, which has two), the south hallway was a disorienting and unforgettable experience.

It was early in our investigation that we named this enigmatic area the Portal Hallway, and the spirits agreed. For those who may not know, a *portal* is an energetic doorway between the physical and nonphysical (some say spiritual) realms where the partition between them is particularly thin. It can also be a doorway between parallel universes. We believe that the north and south hallways, each with a window at the end, acted together to produce an opening between dimensions that allowed spirits to come and go with ease.

According to the ancient Chinese art of *feng shui* (translated as "wind-water"), which is a method and philosophy for harmonizing energy movement and object placement for the spaces we inhabit,

111

The Portal Hallway.

mirrors should not be placed facing each other, because it creates a constant state of bouncing, chaotic energy that is "bad *feng shui.*" Many paranormal researchers believe that this chaos creates a portal.

Tonya had a client during the weeks we were finalizing this book who had three mirrors in her bedroom, all facing toward her bed. The client brought Tonya into her home because she was experiencing sleep paralysis and was getting nightly visits from interdimensionals. Tonya's suggestion to cover the mirrors at night—thereby closing the portal at the intersection of where the mirrors were facing—solved the problem. In the case of the Webb, the windows acted like mirrors, with this same portal effect. We discuss this more in Chapter 18, which lays out the reasons why we believe the Webb is so haunted.

Many of the mediums and sensitives who joined our investigation got the sense of large numbers of spirits coming and going in the Portal Hallway, and our data bore this out. Joey referred to the hallway as "Grand Central Station" after the busy transportation hub in New York City. It would often feel "crowded" although there were only a handful of living people present.

Tonya discovered that the facial recognition feature on a smartphone was a great tool for gathering physical evidence of these large gatherings of spirits in the south hallway. This feature produces a box or a diamond in the camera frame when a face is in focus. One particularly active night, a guest pointed his smartphone camera down what should have been an empty hallway and got nine diamonds on his facial recognition software, followed by patterns of three to five diamonds that we watched appear and disappear in different places on the screen. We heard many random voices on the P-SB11 as this was happening. Other guests captured upward of 20 orbs on their smartphones and cameras.

Several spirits were seen on an old bench along the eastern wall on different nights. Before the bench was placed there, a mother and daughter occupied two chairs for several weeks until the chairs were moved.

Not only was the south hallway crowded with spirits, the energy often felt like it was swirling around, creating a vortex that affected the body and creating feelings of heaviness, light-headedness, nausea, disorientation, and being off balance. Guests described the south hallway as "being on a slant," as though they were in a film with "Dutch angles," where the camera is tilted to evoke a feeling of disorientation, mental illness, or an alternate reality. The EMF meters were most likely to register a high level of activity or for voices to come through the P-SB11 when they were held close to the ceiling. This was the only area in the Webb where this was true.

On numerous occasions we heard banging downstairs and things being moved in rooms on the second floor while we were in the Portal Hallway. This area amplified all the paranormal activity happening in the Webb. Guests were sometimes touched in the Portal Hallway. One night a guest's leg was touched just as we heard on the P-SB11, "It's me!"

One evening in August 2016, the disorientation was producing the worst nausea Joey had ever experienced in the Webb—and it had at times been severe elsewhere on the second floor. A voice on the P-SB11 said, "Portal." We asked how many people were in the hallway and numerous voices said, "Ten." We asked them what they were doing, and they replied, "Don't wanna talk about it" and "No talk."

About a week later the temperature on one of the guns rose from 77 to 83 degrees. The 15 people in the group all remarked on the area feeling hot and one sensitive felt there was someone nearby who had been in a fire. Tonya sensed it as well. The next night Tonya saw a man in a World War II uniform sitting in one of the chairs beneath the window. One of the guests asked Tonya where he was and a voice on the P-SB11 said, "Right here."

The fact that the spirit was in a World War II uniform is important to the sensation of heat and fire from the night before. During the war, the hospital across the street had a burn ward for victims of the oil tankers that were the targets of U-boats on the Crystal Coast. The ward was overseen by Dr. Benjamin Franklin Royal, whose offices were on the south end of the first floor of the Webb. Chapter 14 details our series of encounters with the spirit of a German U-boat captain. Local historians and former library staff, backed up by various documents, told us that the Webb served as a triage and at times burn ward for these victims. Our encounters with burn victims are reported throughout this book.

On another night Tonya sensed a spirit with a wounded or amputated arm. She and Joey both got a sharp metallic taste in their mouths as she saw him.

In the spring of 2017 we met a spirit in uniform who said he was an ensign in the US Navy. The EMF meters stayed consistently in the mid-range while he was with us. In mid-summer the ensign returned on three separate occasions. The third time, he gave us a ping on the P-SB11 (as from a submarine sonar) in the kitchen to let us know that he was in the Portal Hallway. Tonya said he was disappointed that we did not acknowledge him when we were exploring the area, so we went to see him, which made him happy.

Joey and a guest became nauseated on the night of September 30, 2016, an evening when the activity on the second floor started to go to a new and sometimes dangerous level that was sustained for the next year, as we relate in the chapters that follow.

We are noting the date in this case because the nausea and start of the heightened activity could be partially explained by the presence of a UFO mere blocks from the Webb the following night, as reported to MUFON (the Mutual UFO Network). "Hold on," you might be saying, "how could a sighting the following day account for activity *the night before*?" Good question. As we discuss in later chapters, we collected enough data at the Webb to say with surety that linear time (past, present, future) broke down on occasion within its walls, and that conditions found in the realm of quantum physics often best explained some of the phenomena that we experienced. It could also be as simple as the fact that the UFO *was* present on September 30 but was not formally reported.

According to the MUFON database, an attendee of the annual seafood festival (September 30 was the first night of the well-attended event, which takes place in near proximity to the Webb), saw "pulsating [green] lights" about 1,000 feet in the sky "just sitting and pulsating perfectly still." A few minutes later, the lights "move[d] slowly to the left then right about the coast" (a few blocks from the Webb). They then "brightened to a brilliant red for 30 seconds, then returned to pulsating green and kept moving in different directions…" [The UFO] headed out "to sea at a very high rate of speed."

It was not long after that we had our encounters with phantom Men in Black at the Webb (see Chapter 16).

Later in the autumn we were investigating the Portal Hallway and a guest said, "I don't like the feel of this hallway." On the P-SB11 a deep, echo-y male voice replied, "Fuck you!" Soon after, also on the spirit box, we heard, "It's a portal." On evenings that followed we heard, "Portal" and "Check the portal."

One night in July 2017, the Portal Hallway created an optical illusion. It seemed wider than usual to the four of us who had been there before. Some of the guests felt that it widened and narrowed as it was perceived from the area by the stairs. Later in the evening they felt it had changed to a uniform width.

On a night when the Portal Hallway was particularly active, a temperature gun dropped eight degrees, from 82 to 74; we heard eight different voices through the P-SB11; and the EMF meters were all spiking to red. Four named spirits communicated that night: Rachel, Edgar, Walter, and Michael.

On another active night there were several spirits being sensed. "What is your name?" we asked. We heard through the spirit box, "Troy," "There is a portal," and "Work" (which was sung rather than spoken). We asked, "Who is here?" We heard, "Musica" and "Catch a ghost." We also heard, "Voice," "Wassup," and "Yo!" The singing, "musica," and modern expressions all point to John, who is usually in the Cannon Room (see Chapter 16). On a different evening we heard, "What's up, ladies!" Joey asked if it was John and another male voice replied, "It was."

Another spirit we encountered in the Portal Hallway as well as in the Cannon Room was Jacob. We learned from one of Tonya's clients who had visited the Webb during the day and spoken to a staff member that Jacob was a name that at least one child used when asking parents if they could bring one of the spirits home with them.

One evening, a medium sensed a "machine oiler" (someone who operated machinery) in the hallway. Tonya and other sensitives had seen similar spirits on the second floor. We believe they took care of the machines for the garment training facility. We talk about a worker spirit wearing an apron in Chapter 14.

In general, the wide array of voices—male and female; different accents, including an Irish brogue as well as different languages such as French; ethnic names such as Pedro; young and old; kind and harsh— tells us many different types of spirits inhabit and pass through the Webb.

Some of the random communications we heard on the P-SB11 in the Portal Hallway were, "What they said it was," "Question," "Ricky," "Who," "Barry," a male voice that said "Tonya," "You know it's heavy," "Heavy" (two times), "Knowledge," "No," "Whatya know," "You come," and "Don't worry about it."

One of Joey's favorite communications came on a night when we had about a dozen drunk firemen and their wives and girlfriends join the investigation as a surprise birthday gift from one of the fireman's wives. As they walked down the Portal Hallway a spirit on the P-SB11 wryly predicted, "Hangover tomorrow." Another wry remark was heard by a number of us when one of our guest investigators coughed; "Excuse you" came through the P-SB11.

One night in mid-August 2017 the Portal Hallway was particularly lively, with sensitives saying they saw spirits going back and forth at a high rate of speed. The EMF meters were spiking red and we were getting five- to seven-degree temperature drops, most strongly near the ceiling. A voice on the P-SB11 said, "I see the ghosts."

We have mentioned the chairs beneath the window at the end of the hallway. It was not at all unusual for one or two male or female spirits to inhabit them on any given night. In early September 2017 a guest reported being brushed against in the hallway, and right after that Tonya saw an old woman settling into one of the chairs. We frequently encountered elderly spirits sitting there, often wearing housecoats or hospital gowns, which makes sense, given that the hospital and nursing home are just across the street (and a wing of the nursing home remains). Tonya met an Esther or Ethel in one of the chairs. She was wearing a shawl. She saw a grey-haired woman named Selena, who told her she had been in the nursing home across the street. At times sensitives and mediums sensed "confusion" from the elderly spirits sitting in the chairs. One night we encountered an older lady who looked confused to the sensitives who saw her. They felt that it was not dementia but that she was surprised to see us and not sure where she was.

Perhaps the most personal story in the Portal Hallway is that of "Francis," who was an octogenarian in a hospital gown. Tonya saw him sitting at the end of the Portal Hallway one night. He seemed either confused or medicated and she could not tell if he was deceased or having an out-of-body or near-death experience. Two nights later, Tonya returned with two clairaudients to the spot where Francis sat and he told them that he was "looking for my wife." They returned to talk to him later in the evening and he said he knew how to cross over but would not—he was waiting for his wife, who was in the nursing home across the street. He was watching over her because "no one else is." "When she is ready," he told them, they would cross over together. Several days later he moved to a downstairs chair in the Back Stacks to feel closer to her. During our fourth visit with him, he stood and touched a senior member of our group, who wore a portable oxygen tank.

There was a residual haunting of a man in a chair along the east wall of the Portal Hallway. He wore a three-piece green wool suit and sported a red beard. He was seen by Tonya and several other mediums and sensitives.

In early February 2018 we experienced one of the most active nights ever in the Portal Hallway. We heard the name "Paul" three times on the P-SB11 (the repeating of names in a brief amount of time is rare); there was a distinct cold spot in the center of the hallway strong enough to feel through our shoes and pants; Tonya saw a hand by her face (not in her mind's eye, but a disembodied hand floating in front of her); and the EMF spiked consistently red at shoulder level and above. Tonya also saw spirits sitting in four of the five chairs.

Two weeks later, five of six chairs were occupied by a group of spirits chatting happily among themselves—oblivious to us—as, just above their heads, a skeletal creature crawled along the hallway ceiling (see the next chapter for more about this entity). Tonya saw the group and creature as being in separate dimensions. If you count ours as a third, that is quite a lot in a small space!

Our experiences with Vincent and other angry spirits in the north hallway and kitchen led to the establishment of a routine. When our investigation of the Portal Hallway was finished, Joey went alone or with one or two male guests, if any volunteered, down the hall to the northern end, asking if any spirits were present and gauging their mood and openness to contact. A few weeks into this ritual, voices from the P-SB11 said, "Wait" and "Don't move" when Joey tried three times to walk down the Portal Hallway. After that night we often heard, "Stop" or "Wait" as he began his nightly walk toward the north hallway and kitchen.

In the next chapter we discuss at length the curmudgeonly spirit named Vincent and the difficult group of angry male spirits that congregated in the north hallway and kitchen in the summer and fall of 2017.

13
My Name is God
The North Hallway and Kitchen

Without question, the "darkest" areas of the Webb, in terms of the quality of the energy and the personalities/appearance of the entities we encountered, were the north hallway and the kitchen.

Before we detail our experiences with these dark entities, it is important to talk a little about the term "demon." In our various investigations and in places we have lived, we have encountered what we categorize as "demons." We talked about some of these encounters in Chapter 1. They can be deeply unsettling. These encounters involve nonhuman entities that clearly intend disruption and harm.

We encountered only one possible "demon" in the classic mythological or religious sense in the Webb. In July 2016, on a night when Joey led an investigation on his own, out of the P-SB11 he and the guests heard the word "demon" spoken in the north hallway. Around this same time (and without any communication between them) Tonya woke up at home and felt like she was on fire. The thought that entered her mind was, "There's a demon in the Webb."

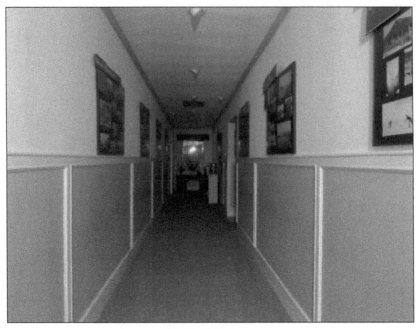

The North Hallway.

As for the spirits that were unfriendly and at times angry, we are convinced that, almost without exception (and we are clear about the exceptions throughout the book), they were once human and, for a variety of reasons, they held on to their anger after death.

In the last chapter we mentioned a spirit named Vincent who gave us more than a little trouble for the first year or so of our investigation. We now come to the logical place in our story to recount our experiences with him in detail.

From the first night we entered the Webb with the owner of Port City, we received angry, insulting communications from a spirit that Tonya could see was male. At first we knew him only as "the Foreman," after an impression Tonya got that he was the man who oversaw the garment training facility upstairs. It was a label he did not like. A few weeks into the investigation Tonya referred to him as the Foreman and he asked on the P-SB11, "What did you just call me?" Early on he said that his name was "Woody," which turned out to be false, and he called any female who entered the north hallway a "bitch" or "whore." Even when we weren't in the north hallway, he stood in it and glared at us,

120

beaming a negative energy so intense that those who could not see him could easily feel his presence.

We learned Vincent's name through a series of communications on the P-SB11 from both male and female spirits. This trend of spirits—especially female spirits—speaking for or about Vincent was one that continued up until our last encounters with him.

Vincent targeted Tonya from the outset, although she stood up to him one evening several months into our investigation when she felt he crossed the line. As he stood in near proximity to her, growling, she said to him, sternly but calmly, "Don't you growl at me." This exchange signaled the first turn in what became a fascinating relationship.

You see, one of the many things that we learned in the 150-plus hours we spent investigating the Webb was that spirits display all the same emotions and range of personality types as when they were human. During our first open-to-the-public investigation in May 2016 a diviner and shaman who was with us referred to Vincent as the "grumpy uncle" of a large family of spirits. We took this wisdom to heart in all our encounters with Vincent and then with the angry male spirits we report on in detail later in the chapter. Over the course of that summer, Tonya left Vincent a variety of essential oils and healing stones, in the hopes that they would help him.

Each evening throughout that first summer, we had experiences of some sort with Vincent, whom we still knew only as "the Foreman." We had also heard various bits of story and gossip about him. The most prevalent—backed up by what we were experiencing—was that he was a bully with "happy hands" who took advantage of the women under his supervision. Vincent spoke the name of one of the former female guides who had told us about him on a few different occasions. He wondered why she was no longer around. He had managed to bully her to the point that one night she and another female leading the tour closed it down early and left in such a hurry they had to call the tour owner to go to the Webb to turn off the lights and lock the doors.

Interacting with Vincent took us into the kitchen off the end of the north hallway, where we sensed he stayed most of the time. It is hard to describe the uneasy feeling of that area. It felt oppressive. Just past the kitchen was a storage and small office area. There was also a skinny closet. One night, Tonya got a glimpse of a male figure scurrying into the closet and then into a hole in the ceiling. We had discovered Vincent's "hidey hole." Some nights the oppressive feeling in that kitchen/office area was so strong that Joey's head hurt and he dry heaved—a sure sign for him of the presence of strong electromagnetic energy (the World Health Organization has labeled the effects of exposure to EMF that some people experience "electromagnetic sensitivity").

One evening, as Joey scanned the area before letting guests in, he felt as though a hand tightened around his throat, enough to make him gag. He exited into the hallway and did not allow anyone into the area that night.

By the middle of our first summer, as we tried to forge a relationship with Vincent, we felt like his anger was softening; that we were, for lack of a better word, becoming "acquaintances" rather than intruders; but at the end of July, after several nights of calm, he resumed his cursing and screaming in Tonya's face and in the face of one of the sensitives in the group.

Soon after the resumption of his bullying, he revealed some details about the end of his life—his loneliness and despair—and showed Tonya an injury to his neck, perhaps from a rope he used to hang himself, which might explain the feeling Joey had in the kitchen of having his throat gripped and tightened, and which other guests felt in the hallways (see Chapter 11).

Vincent's moods fluctuated wildly throughout the rest of the summer. When he was in a bad mood or felt like we had overstayed our welcome on the second floor, he caused physical sensations: dizziness, nausea, and the tightening feeling in the throat or under the jawline. We did not think he was trying to physically hurt us. Rather, the injury to his neck was so painful that he constantly identified with it and used it as a "tool" for communicating his discomfort to us. It was an empathic connection that allowed us to feel the pain as he did. When he was at his angriest, groups clearly sensed someone glaring at them. From the beginning, Vincent stood outside the door of the Meeting Room and made his contempt known to us.

One night, Joey asked him, as he always did, if we could enter his space. "No," he said (all communications from or about Vincent were through the P-SB11 unless otherwise noted). Joey asked how he was feeling and he responded, "Awful." Another night he said he was "okay," "better," and then said, "Sorry." Several nights later he yelled, "Bitch!"

122

The next night Tonya asked how he felt. He said, "Very good," but he was making Joey feel nauseated.

A female voice a few nights later said, "Vincent" two times. Two nights after that a male voice said, "Vincent" and the next night a woman's voice said, "Vincent." Joey said he thought she was acting as his protector. Vincent immediately responded, "Bullshit."

Two nights after that Joey asked Vincent if it would be okay to bring people into his area. He said, "Yes." Joey asked again and Vincent said, "Okay." We proceeded down the north hallway. Joey's heart clenched and another paranormal researcher felt a strong, heavy presence. Tonya asked Vincent about 10 feet into the hallway if we could come closer. He said, "No. Fuck you." We promptly turned around.

One night in August 2016, Joey could not join the investigation, so a young investigator we were mentoring took his place. As he walked down the north hallway ahead of the rest of the group, Vincent asked, "You're taking over?" When the fill-in investigator asked if the group could speak with him, he said, "I don't give a fuck." Under those circumstances, the group did not approach Vincent's area. The next night, Joey made his way down the north hallway and said, "Hi, Vincent, it's Joey." To which Vincent asked, "Are you?"

Females often reported being pinched, poked, touched, or tickled in the north hallway during our period of contact with Vincent. Three female guests at various times reported being touched on the left calf. Another woman reported that she was touched several times on the second floor; she later got what felt like a "hot flash" in the Intro Room at the end of the night. Everyone else in the room (seven of us) was cool and comfortable. On another night, while we were near the kitchen door, one of the guests reported that the jacket tied around her waist was pulled down. She had to untie it to release it from around her ankles, so it didn't fall on its own. At the same time, two other female guests reported being touched on the back of the neck.

At the end of September 2016, as we reached the landing at the top of the second floor stairs, a female voice said, "Vincent's not here." Actually, he was, and he was particularly upset that night, cursing and saying "Go!" Several nights later Vincent's female "protector" said, "Vincent's here." His presence was strong. Several people felt it. But he stayed silent.

In early October 2016, in the hallway leading to Vincent's room, a spirit asked, "Who's this?" Joey identified himself. We heard, "Hi" and "Vincent." Joey called out to Vincent, who replied, "What?" That night, Vincent was agitated and was hanging from the ceiling over the kitchen table to display his displeasure at how the other spirits were willing to communicate with us. A medium joining us that night saw a dark-haired spirit in Vincent's area.

A few weeks later, Joey headed toward Vincent's area. He asked, "Vincent, are you here?" Vincent: "Yes." Joey: "Can I bring people?" Vincent: "Yes." As we were leaving Vincent's area, a male voice, not Vincent's, said, "You guys are punks." This may have been the bathroom spirit from downstairs or a hint at the congregation of angry male spirits that was to develop in the coming months.

A former guest reported to us through an email over a year after she first visited, just after falling and breaking her nose, that she had a dream that Vincent came to her and put cold compresses on her face. The email came just a day after Halloween, when we had done a special investigation preceded by a lecture in which we talked about Vincent and his journey from bully to redeemed.

From that time on, we heard from Vincent less and less, until, by the end of May 2017, we received no contact from him at all. We do not know if he crossed over, or if he is still in the Webb, but remaining there in such a way that he became unknown to us. We hope that he has found some peace. He was certainly one of the most unique "characters" we have ever encountered.

And it has become clear to us that, although he did not like the label of "the Foreman," that was truly what he was among the spirits on the second floor. Once he was gone, things took a turn for the dark and difficult in the north hallway and kitchen. It became the gathering place for a group of angry male spirits that made their presence known with clarity and authority through the summer and well into the fall. And, as you will see in Chapter 16, about the Cannon Room, for some nonhuman entities as well.

As with Vincent, we do not believe these spirits meant us any harm (most of them, anyway) or were in any way "demonic." They were simply personalities that wanted to be left alone and not be intruded upon, and they "staked out" that area of the Webb as their own for many months. These spirits put the temperature gauge on the P-SB11 into the blue and drained the batteries or otherwise jammed the spirit box to keep us from communicating with them or any other spirits. On numerous occasions they froze cameras and cell phones.

Before things intensified with the angry spirits, we had an experience with a nonhuman entity, an interdimensional, on Memorial Day weekend of 2017. Jerry, the gambler we met in the Intro Room, was acting as a protector for Tonya upstairs that night. As we approached the kitchen, Jerry called out through the P-SB11, "Be careful!" Joey and three other guests became nauseated or had an ill feeling when they approached the area. In the kitchen it was particularly bad. Several people, including Tonya, would not go in there—she and one of the guests who was a sensitive both saw a "creature" was present beyond the doorway.

Jerry motioned urgently to Tonya that Joey and a female guest who had gone into the kitchen should get out. Before she could convey the message, a sinister-sounding voice came through the P-SB11 in the kitchen and they left the kitchen on their own.

Later in the evening, as we closed the investigation in the Intro Room, Tonya and the guest both described this creature as hairy with a round bottom. It looked like something out of a Maurice Sendak book. It had sharp teeth and claws and prominent ears that were pointed and stood straight up, and it had a nasty energy about it that the illustration does not fully capture.

Tonya's sketch of the interdimensional.

It is interesting to note that the shape of the interdimensional is similar to the shadow in the photo of Joey and Robby outside the Webb in Chapter 4.

Joey really wanted to make contact with the interdimensional and went upstairs by himself with the P-SB11 after the investigation. But—and he reports this with no shame—the hackles that went up all over his body were fierce and he got frightened. As he walked down the north hallway toward the kitchen he heard a distinct sound like an animal was expelling all the air from its lungs—deep and guttural. He heard, "Hold it" on the P-SB11. He quickly went downstairs, having not made it anywhere near the kitchen door.

After the sighting of the interdimensional, the Webb had an unexplained flea infestation.

Back to the very human, very angry, male spirits. At one point in early August things were so difficult in this area that we no longer approached it from the hallway, from which we often received angry warnings, but instead investigated the Piano Room, which has a doorway directly across from the kitchen. From there we "tested the waters." On most nights, we were warned away or otherwise felt a presence so intense and unfriendly that we left the north hallway and the kitchen/storage area beyond it alone.

One night, while we were doing just that, a guest reported a presence outside the Piano Room door, directly across from the kitchen, and a male voice said on the P-SB11, "That ain't cool." A guest then saw a shadow move across the Meeting Room door down the hall. It was solid enough to block out the lights from windows behind it and it moved at a slow, deliberate pace.

In the Piano Room on a night soon after Joey and a guest both had simultaneous physical reactions as the group approached the door across from the kitchen. Joey's nerve endings were lit up from his face to his feet. The guest said he felt like his back suddenly tensed up and needed to be cracked.

As we approached the kitchen one night in early June, when the atmosphere in the north hallway seemed calmer, Joey felt nauseated; the energy was suddenly heavy. We heard, "Vincent" and "Get out of the way" on the P-SB11. Two weeks later, Joey and two male guests walked down the north hallway toward the kitchen. Approaching the door, they heard, "Whoa." One of the men was a police officer who said he went into immediate "alert." He said that if he had had his gun he would have placed his hand on it. The other guest got goose bumps on his arms and legs. Joey asked, "Can I bring people in?" A female voice replied, "No people." Joey went further down the hallway. A woman's voice said, "Oh, forget it" and then he heard, "Whoa, boy" as he turned back toward the group to let them know we were staying away from that area.

During the height of the difficulty with the angry male spirits we heard near the kitchen, "Stay away from the door." Guests reported hearing what some described as a bark and others as a growl.

Things got so difficult at one point in the summer that we considered suspending the public investigations. Although we were joined by a good number of mediums and paranormal investigators with prior experience and some energetic practices to keep themselves protected, most of our guests were vacationers who were either curious or just out for a good time. But no one wants to be yelled at, feel nauseated, or be called ugly names. After a good deal of conversation, we decided to continue, with some further adjustments.

First, we decided to start the investigation upstairs, as activity and negative energy tended to increase the longer we were in the Webb. Sure enough, on the first night, things were calm at the top of the stairs. Before we had a chance to pat ourselves on the back, however, we realized that the angry spirits had congregated downstairs because we had started upstairs! Their anger was more diffuse downstairs, but they still jammed the P-SB11 after sending the temperature gauge into the blue. Joey dropped his equipment bag in the Intro Room before joining everyone in the Children's Room and heard the bag drop *a second time* as he was leaving. Outside the Children's Room a voice on the P-SB11 said, "Go away." Joey heard the same thing in the same place a few nights later.

Another night, when we were deciding which room to venture into next from the start of the north hallway, a voice from the P-SB11 said, "Get out." Tonya asked, "What room should we go to next?" and the reply was, "Just get out."

Joey went to the kitchen door a few nights later, and the area felt calm. He asked if he could bring people in and was told, "No" and "Hang it up." Outside the kitchen several nights later the P-SB11 jammed after we heard several unintelligible, but clearly angry, male voices. Joey asked, "Who is this?" The reply was, "The box." We also heard, "Shut up." During another visit we heard, "Anger spot," "Judgment," "Noir," and "Cross over." Ironically, we also heard, "Come back," which may have been a taunt.

On a night with a lot of activity, a wildlife camera was malfunctioning in the upstairs hallway and a camera someone was using to take a picture of the doorway to the kitchen would not work. Two sensitives were getting the message to "stay away."

One evening when Tonya was out of town and Jolie was filling in, one of the male spirits from our house that accompanied Jolie on her visits to the Webb was confronted by three male spirits, one of whom was pulling his own hair with both hands and screaming like the figure in the famous Edvard Munch painting. Another paranormal group who was investigating the Webb the next night reported on their Facebook page that it was "active and emotional."

The following week, a teenage sensitive was pulled from the north hallway toward the Cannon Room (most likely by the spirit named John). On the way she asked Tonya if we could go into any room. Tonya said that as long as the door was open we could go in. A voice on the P-SB11 said, "Not one door." The male spirit waited several seconds and repeated the phrase. We were sure he meant the kitchen door, so we did not go near it that night.

The energy in early August was so heavy upstairs that one sensitive burst into tears and three people got nauseated. The oppressive energy was so strong one night soon after that we explored and left the upstairs as quickly as possible. As we were leaving the building a guest sensed someone behind a locked office door. Tonya heard a high-pitched release of energy and the P-SB11 temperature gauge went to blue, indicating an angry spirit. We heard music and a deep voice said, "Yeah."

At the end of August, one of the angry spirits shared his name, which was Ron. He said things on the P-SB11 like, "On the lamb," "Goddammit," "Bullshit," "That bitch," "Bitch," and "Mad material." Tonya and a fellow medium named Bryon felt as though Ron was angry because he died too soon. Bryon felt Ron wanted to talk to us about it. When we tried he said, "Silent"—but there was a large group of guest investigators that night. The next night Ron was in the Meeting Room. Joey tried to communicate with him. Ron answered, "I said, 'Fuck you,'" but then added, "This is Ron." We tried on other nights but received no further communications from him.

Around this time in August, Jolie saw a skeletal figure crawling on the ceiling in the north hallway by the kitchen. It was confirmed by Tonya. Another sensitive saw it the next night as a spider. Bryon saw it a few weeks later and described the sound of bones "clicking" as it moved across the ceiling. In early September 2017 Jolie again saw the skeletal figure crawling along the ceiling. In mid-October it was crawling on the ceiling in the Cannon Room.

In mid-August, as we were leaving the Cannon Room, we heard on the P-SB11, "Showing off, kids?" After most of the group of 12 went downstairs Joey stayed behind with two guests to see if activity picked up, since the kitchen area was quiet earlier in the evening. Joey mentioned going into the kitchen and heard on the P-SB11, "If you must." One of the guests said that she got a panicked feeling by one of the closed doors at the top of the stairs. The three of them rejoined the group. As everyone was leaving Dr. T's room at the end of the investigation, the two guests who stayed with Joey upstairs stayed behind again. They all heard, "Keep walking."

It was also on an evening in August that the angry male spirits decided they were not content to just target the living. When we first climbed the stairs Joey heard an emotional, pleading female voice on the P-SB11. He immediately knew who it was, and his heart rate increased.

Although it was rare for children to be seen or heard on the second floor, there had been two instances over the summer when a little girl had been seen there (a male child was in the Meeting Room in mid-April 2018 as well, although he did not communicate with us). She told us her name was Rachel. She was 10 years old and wore a white dress. One sensitive saw her playing with a ball. The second night we encountered her, she was posing like a ballerina, which was caught on camera by one of our guests (although we requested a copy of the photo, we never received one). Joey is usually the most skeptical about images caught on camera, as they are almost always explained away as tricks of light, but this image was so clear it is hard to refute.

Back to the evening in August. After hearing Rachel's distressed voice on the P-SB11 at the top of the stairs, we all heard it just outside the Meeting Room. Tonya agreed that it was Rachel, who said, "Help!"

and "Let's get out of here." We encouraged her to follow us down the stairs and to stay with us. As we got halfway down the second set of stairs a male voice said, "Don't screw with her." Tonya took most of the guests into the Children's Room. Joey monitored the P-SB11 near the stairs to see if Rachel would continue to communicate. As Joey walked next to the banister both he and a male guest who stayed with him heard a loud THUD from upstairs. They went upstairs to investigate and found nothing in any room knocked over or moved. They did not go near the kitchen. As a matter of fact, Joey could make it only halfway down the north hallway before the nausea and hackles were so severe he had to turn back.

The next week, Rachel screamed through the P-SB11 while we were in the Cannon Room. We entered the north hallway. Joey asked for her by name and she said, "Yes" on the P-SB11. Joey then "saw her" (it was a strong intuitional knowing rather than a clear visual image) surrounded by the angry male spirits. We managed to get her to come down the hallway toward us. The older woman whom we believe protected and spoke for Vincent a year earlier said, "She got away." We asked Rachel to come downstairs with us. As we gathered in the Children's Room to catch our breath after bringing Rachel to Dr. T for protection, we heard an angry male voice ask, "Where is she?" When we went back into Dr. T's room he and Rachel were gone. Joey went to the stairs to see if there was any activity and a male voice called him a "rat."

Two nights later, Rachel was still with Dr. T. We did not encounter her upstairs the next week. In early September we heard Rachel moaning as we went up the stairs. We could not find her anywhere upstairs and she did not communicate again that night. As Joey went down the hallway toward the kitchen looking for her he heard, "Nope" and "Careful" on the P-SB11. He turned back. As we regrouped in the Piano Room we stood in the doorway looking into the kitchen and Joey asked, "How many of you are there?" The spirits answered, "Enough."

The next night, Rachel did not speak, but her cries were chilling. We did a thorough search of the upstairs rooms and could not locate her. As we told the guests about Rachel's history with us, a deep male voice on the P-SB11 said, "Cry." A female said, "Probably."

In the Meeting Room a few minutes later, Joey looked through his field notes for the specifics about our prior encounters with Rachel to share with the guests. He wondered aloud as he flipped pages if it was in July. A voice from the P-SB11 said, "Afterward." The spirit was right—our experiences with Rachel, as you just read, were in August.

In late August there was a black, shapeless mass seen in the north hallway as we sat in the Meeting Room. Someone was also staring at us from the hallway, giving one guest chills.

By late September, things had settled down upstairs and although there were some sharp male voices around the kitchen area, there were no warnings or indication that several angry spirits were still gathered together. Why they had left—or were much calmer—is as mysterious as what gathered and enraged them in the first place.

Things got more active upstairs in early October. Near the entrance to the kitchen one night we heard, "Just keep walking, buddy" and "Jerk." A different male voice added, "Think about it." At the top of the stairs about a week later a male voice said, "Just stay there." A female voice responded, "Don't lecture me."

On a night soon after we heard, "Do you mind?" When a male guest entered the hallway by himself (something we discouraged guests from doing) we heard a threatening male voice say, "Maaaaannnnnn." Joey went to get the guest and we heard, "Don't leave the room." A woman asked if she could take the spirit's picture and he replied, "NO." When we went downstairs one of the guests said of the angry spirit, "I want to poke him" and we heard, "Stay down" followed by "Bitch."

During an investigation in early December Jolie saw a grey, wraithlike figure crawling on the ceiling in the north hallway (which might have been the wraith reported in an earlier chapter). When we first went down the hallway it wasn't there but later it re-appeared and followed us. That same night, Jolie saw a trickster figure, like the Native American *heyokah*, dressed in black and trying to pass for human, motioning with long fingers for Joey to follow him into the kitchen as Joey stood in the doorway of the Piano Room. The spirit got angry with Jolie when she warned Joey about what the spirit was trying to do.

In early February 2018, things were much calmer. As Joey walked ahead of everyone else down the north hallway a friendly male voice said, "Hello, sir!" The only other contact we had was in the storage/office area behind the kitchen when a voice on the P-SB11 said, "Workers."

The kitchen entrance taken from the Piano Room.

Despite everything we reported in this chapter, perhaps the most unsettling communication we ever received on the P-SB11 in the north hallway was the one we used for the title of this chapter, "My name is God." We say "unsettling" because there was never any indication who the spirit was that said it, or if he believed it to be true. We will say that it did not sound at all like a jest.

If it was a god of some kind (whatever that might mean), we are grateful it did not choose to demonstrate its power.

14
Don't Cross the Line
The Piano Room

After all the excitement and activity of the hallways and kitchen area, we took the opportunity to bring the group to a much calmer room to catch our breath and reflect on whatever we experienced thus far that night. Of course, in the summer of 2017, with one of the doors to the Piano Room facing the kitchen area where the angry male spirits were congregated, a breather was rarely what we got.

As we stood in the doorway facing the kitchen one night, a shadow of a man appeared in front of the east-facing kitchen window; Tonya saw the shadow in the Piano Room. As we entered the Piano Room a month later, Tonya and a guest looked back and saw a shadow pass in front of a plant outside the nearby Cannon Room. Our field notes are full of mentions of guests seeing shadows outside that room.

Sometimes the shadows seen from the Piano Room were lures to get us into the hallways. One night a teen reported feeling a persistent pain in his shoulder, as if it was pulling him toward the door. On another night, everyone in the group was psychically pulled to the door opposite the kitchen. Numerous people simultaneously got chills.

133

We often got brief snippets of communication in the Piano Room without getting details like names or other contextual information. Some of the communications through the P-SB11 were "Was that amusing," "How you doing," "How is it going," and "Wanna see?" In the last case we replied, "Yes." "Turn out the lights," they said. When we did, someone saw movement outside the door opposite the kitchen.

One night when everyone was being pulled to the door opposite the kitchen, Joey went to it with the P-SB11 and got a sick feeling in his solar plexus. Hackles went up on his arms, back, and neck. Out of the P-SB11 came, "Warning," "Steve," "Wanna talk," "The Scripture," "Hello," "The music," and "Hello" again in a deeper male voice than the first one—all in rapid succession.

The temperature gauge on the P-SB11 went to blue in the Piano Room one night. Guests felt a pull back to the kitchen from the doorway. We got some EMF spikes at the same time. Joey went back into the kitchen and a luring male voice said, "Over here."

One night when the interactions with the angry spirits were particularly difficult we heard, "At the door" while investigating the Piano Room. Joey went to the door opposite the kitchen, but no one was there. A few minutes later a guest stated that she had sneaked into the hall and had been by the door when the message came through.

Another night, outside the kitchen but still in the Piano Room, we heard on the P-SB11, "Just your door" and "Don't cross the line." We said that we were leaving soon, and paired voices said, "The odds are pretty good."

A night soon after, as Joey and a male guest stepped through the door into the Piano Room, they heard an angry male voice and the P-SB11 went to blue. They immediately closed the door. The P-SB11 jammed and would not turn on. A female guest said she heard chattering voices from beyond the door.

In early fall 2016, while standing in the Piano Room, an investigator was noticeably unsettled. He heard the name "Randall" spoken in the room. His exact quote was, "I'ma 'bout ready to get on outta here."

The angry male spirits were not the only ones who contacted us in the Piano Room. A woman named "Elizabeth" was sensed one night. As we approached the piano, a voice on the P-SB11 said, "I'll play." We heard no music however.

Another night we heard the name "Claudia" on the P-SB11. One of our guests was a music major in college and asked if he could play the piano for the spirits. No one on our investigations had tried before, so we agreed. The spirits did not respond, but the other guests enjoyed the spontaneous mini-concert, as did John in the Cannon Room, as you will read in the next chapter.

On several occasions Tonya saw a group of women in 1920s-style dresses sitting in chairs near the piano. The women were holding drinks and socializing as if at a party or social event. One night a guest investigator managed to capture a photo of the area. What appeared to be a wine glass could clearly be seen floating in the air (this was another instance where the guests said they would send us the photo but didn't).

Another spirit that Tonya saw regularly in the Piano Room was that of a man whose attire was consistent with a Mennonite's. Tonya always saw him sitting at the same table intently reading his Bible.

An African American man, perhaps from the 1800s, was seen by a sensitive in two different areas of the room. He appeared to be sad. Several weeks later, a guest sensed a heavy sadness in the same area. About a week later Joey felt as if he was going to cry and had to expend considerable effort to hold back tears.

Joey heard Rachel's name on the P-SB11 a few weeks before we had our series of encounters with her (see the two previous chapters).

We set up for our Halloween 2017 presentation in the Piano Room. By that time the activity upstairs had settled down. We thought it best to pick the quietest room in the Webb in terms of paranormal activity in which to do our one-hour lecture, "The Art and Craft of Modern Investigation." As we prepared, we both got strong feelings of pulsing energy in the solar plexus, which caused our legs to wobble. About 15 minutes later Joey turned on the P-SB11 and we got our first communication of the night—a friendly "Hello" from a male. We both said that we were excited to spend time at the Webb on Halloween night. We heard, "We are not." Tonya said that we were going to bring a group of people in and a female voiced answered, excitedly, "Really?"

As we were leaving the Piano Room in early February 2018 we heard a friendly "Goodbye." Earlier that night Tonya had heard the name "Anthony" in her mind while we were in the Back Stacks. As we were investigating the Piano Room, we clearly heard on the P-SB11, "Anthony."

The Piano Room produced physical phenomena. A guest took a video of the chandelier one night and on playback the arms of the fixture were pulsing with energy.

Guests also reported the strong odor of cigar smoke and a flash of light moving from the Piano Room to the Meeting Room.

We have chosen the oddest occurrence in the Piano Room (and one of the oddest in the Webb) with which to end the chapter. One night, Joey reached into his pocket to get his flashlight and felt something wet on his finger. It looked like someone had sneezed all over his left forefinger. His clothes and the table where he sat were dry and he had not sneezed. As a matter of fact, he asked if anyone had heard him sneeze and the P-SB11 said, "Sneeze." When he wiped off the goo, there was considerably more liquid than he would have expected.

Was this some form of ectoplasm? The residue of a spirit's "sneeze"? This is just one of the many lingering questions we have about phenomena inside the Webb Memorial Library and its mysterious second floor.

Epilogue

As we were finalizing this book we received an email from a former volunteer at the library who wanted to talk to us about experiences she has had as a sensitive, including some of the things she witnessed at the Webb. During our meeting, she related that, several years ago, the day before a paranormal investigation group was due at the library, she arrived to learn that the glass face of the clock in the Piano Room and a lamp on a nearby table had been found broken on the floor. The staff had been in the room talking about the visit the day before.

It seems clear that well before and during our time there, spirits in the Webb became angry at the idea of investigators invading their space.

15
Everything is Hot
The Meeting Room

Of all the rooms and hallways in the Webb Memorial Library, the Meeting Room was the most varied in the types of experiences we had. It literally was a meeting room—a large room with a conference table and a comfortable sitting area where large groups of people—or spirits—gathered. It was used in the past for Alcoholics Anonymous meetings. It also must have been a festive and happy room after the renovations in 1936 that made it a key part of the building's re-invention as a civic center.

Given this history, it is no surprise that we often experienced the ghostly echoes of both parties and meetings within its paneled and richly trimmed walls.

One night we encountered a female spirit named Vicky who was from the 1930s. One of our teenage female guests heard jazz music played by horns and a sax. We asked the spirits, "Is this a party?" to which a male replied on the P-SB11, "It is." Another male voice said, "Helloooo." The spirits in attendance told Tonya it was a debutante ball in 1937. Some weeks later our daughter Jolie sensed a party with jazz music. Her hand was touched two times by happy spirits.

The Meeting Room.

On another evening several of us got the distinct impression of a gathering or party. We did not receive any clear communications through the P-SB11. We did, however, get several spikes to the red on the EMF meters when we asked questions about what kind of party it was. After a series of trial and error questions, we were "told" by the strong spikes on the EMF meter that it was a graduation party.

There was a Bible or prayer group in the Meeting Room one night. The air felt so solemn it was like being in a church. We were respectful and did not stay.

On a night in July 2016, as we entered the Meeting Room, we all got a sense that it was filled with spirits all talking at once, as if a meeting of some importance and contention was in progress. This had also been Tonya's experience in the room on her first visit to the Webb in 2015.

We again encountered a meeting a month later. Tonya saw men in black suits sitting around the conference table. They were in heated discussion, finger-pointing and pounding their fists. From the P-SB11 we heard, "Bullshit" and "Asshole," as if the men were throwing insults at each other over their differences of opinion. She was drawn to a book called *Navy*. On page 162, which she was strongly drawn to, was the Cuban Missile Crisis of 1962. She later found a photo online of President Kennedy and his advisors; they wore similar clothing, so the time period matches. Further research eight months later, as we were preparing this book, revealed that Kennedy attended a review of the Navy and Marines stationed half an hour from the Webb in April 1962. It is hard to ignore the similarity of 162/1962.

We asked, "Are there soldiers here?" The response from the P-SB11 was, "Yes, there are." Perhaps it was a logistics meeting for Kennedy's visit, or was related to the Cuban Missile Crisis. The area's navy and marine presence was highly mobilized during that nearly two-week period, and tensions were high.

In early February 2018 we met the spirit of a World War II army soldier at the head of the conference table. We were not surprised, given the Webb was used for triage and at times for a burn ward when German U-boats attacked oil tankers leaving the port in Morehead City. We encountered the spirits of servicemen from that era elsewhere on the second floor.

Of course, the soldier could have been in the Meeting Room for a different reason altogether.

The story we are about to share (which is a sequence of "episodes" over a long period of time) is a clear case of how our varied approach to paranormal investigation—a combination of historical research, mediumship, use of technical equipment, application of the principles of storytelling, and attention to synchronicity—helped us put the pieces together to what is one of the most interesting ongoing experiences we had at the Webb.

It was on a night in the late summer of 2016 that we heard two voices speaking German on the P-SB11 in the Meeting Room. One of our teen guests, who spoke limited German, activated a German app on his phone and one of the voices on the P-SB11 responded to it with simple words and phrases. This happened two more times in the weeks that followed. Each time, when the German came through, someone in the group spoke at least a little of the language.

About a month later we mentioned to our guest investigators that we sometimes received communications in German in the Meeting

Room. There was a music major with us that night who knew a song in German. He sang a few verses. In response, a female voice on the P-SB11 said in English, "I really miss you." Another female voice said, "Cool." We did not receive any German communications that night.

Early in 2017, the mystery of the German voices took an interesting turn when a medium asked, "Who got their leg stuck mid-calf in a U-boat?" This was a synchronicity, as Joey had been doing a lot of research for a story he was creating for an immersive Escape Room project that centered on the German U-boat attacks in North Carolina during World War II (over 300 ships were sunk in the attacks). We received communication in German from the P-SB11 that none of us could understand. Joey and two other guests simultaneously felt dizzy and had stomach pains. A male voice said, "Oooh" on the P-SB11, as if the speaker felt a similar pain.

Two weeks later, we heard a deep male voice say, "Bastard." A male voice spoke German on the P-SB11. Sure enough—one of the guests spoke German and they had a simple conversation. Before they got too far in, the temperature gauge on the P-SB11 showed a drop in temperature and it jammed, a sure sign (based on repeated experience in the Webb) that an angry spirit or spirits did not want the conversation to happen.

That was the last time we heard any German on the P-SB11 for many months. Then, at the end of August, the German language communications resumed. You guessed it—one of the guests spoke a little German. She said, "*Ich liebe dich*" [I love you] and a male voice said, "*Ja*" [yes]. In early September Jolie saw the German spirit. He was dressed in the uniform of a German naval officer and was sitting in one of the chairs. Another guest and Joey spoke some basic German words and phrases. The German officer shook his head, annoyed at our attempts at communication. The EMF meters lit up to red four consecutive times each time Joey said, "*Ich liebe dich*." The German officer crossed the room and put his hands on the table and leaned in over us, spiking the EMF once more to red. He put his arm around Jolie's shoulder and said, sarcastically, "*Danka*" [thank you]. He was annoyed that she had pointed him out to us.

In early December 2017 Jolie again saw the German naval officer. He was standing by the back cabinets, an area where we had been experiencing high EMF readings and other anomalies for months, as you will read about at the end of the chapter. When he saw Joey, he made a *zeig heil,* the Nazi salute. Joey said, *"Guten tag"* [good day]. He gave Joey the finger and said, *"Heil"* [hail] on the P-SB11. Jolie felt like he was showing his nationalism and loyalty to the Nazi cause.

It was at this moment, 18 months or so after first contact, that Joey put most of the pieces together. On a shelf in the Meeting Room was a framed picture of the sunken U-boat 352.

The next morning, Joey researched U-352. It arrived off the coast of the northeastern United States in the spring of 1942 and was sunk on May 9, 1942 by depth charges from the *Icarus,* a Coast Guard cutter, not far from Morehead City. The Coast Guard crew fired machine guns at the survivors and departed, returning less than an hour later to pick up 33 survivors, including U-352's captain, Hellmut Rathke. About a third of the crew died.

According to a declassified August 1942 Office of the Chief of Naval Operations report of the interrogations of the survivors, Rathke kept careful control over his men, advising them how to answer when questioned, reminding them to not divulge secret information, and enforcing strict discipline while they were prisoners of war. U-352 was only on her second cruise and had sunk no ships. The report states that "[Rathke] professes unqualified admiration for Hitler and National Socialism" and that he said Hitler was a "genius at everything." His pride and behavior witnessed by us prior to reading this report is on point with this assessment.

Another interesting bit from the report is that Rathke had suffered a debilitating ski injury to his leg prior to taking command of U-352. He used a wheelchair for a time while a prisoner of war. Perhaps that was the "mid-calf" injury that the medium had sensed.

The story doesn't end there. In the late 1980s, the surviving crew of U-352 held a reunion in the United States not far from where U-352 was sunk. They did not invite their former captain. Instead, they sent a notice of the meeting to Rathke with a strongly worded note that he was not welcome. They went so far as to type up an "indictment" against Rathke for what they perceived as his "crimes." There is a full page in the Naval report of the punishments he gave his men while prisoners of war.

Joey's research included finding photographs of Rathke. Due to copyrights, we are not including the photos but you can easily find them by searching "Hellmut Rathke" on the Internet. As you will see, there are no Nazi insignia or anything else to identify who might be the man in the photos. Joey showed the photos to Jolie and she immediately picked out Rathke, who is in the middle of one of them, as the German she saw in the Meeting Room, although, to her, he appeared in full regalia and clean-shaven. It could be that Rathke's arrogance and pride had him clinging to a lost dream and he wanted to appear to us to have retained his importance. That he haunts a room in a public library about an hour's boat ride from the site of his defeat, captured in a photograph of his sunken U-boat, is compelling on many levels. And the story still goes on.

We told you about a World War II soldier at the head of the conference table in February 2018. His presence led Joey to tell the guests about the German U-boat captain. As Joey finished the story, an angry burst of German came out of the P-SB11. Two weeks later, Tonya saw Rathke for the first time. He was standing in his usual spot by the cabinets. He was smoking and looked exactly like Jolie described him. For months, guests reported smelling cigarette smoke in the Meeting Room, and on several occasions, Tonya saw the vague outline of a spirit sitting in a chair and smoking. One night, a sensitive reported *seeing* the smoke—it could have been Rathke all along. As we settled into the room, he said, "*Zeig heil!*" loud and clear on the P-SB11. Joey spoke to him in his poor German but Rathke just smoked and ignored him. He then jammed the spirit box. When Joey got the spirit box working again, he asked, "Are you *kapitan* of U-352?" Rathke did not answer. Instead he walked to the picture of his sunken U-boat. He was near enough to an EMF meter to spike it to red. He walked to where Joey had left his field notes, some of which were about him. After staring at them for a bit, he moved around the room and touched two women (notably, they had blonde hair and one had blue eyes—the other had green). Just like our prior engagement with him, Rathke ended the night with an angry burst of German. He then disappeared.

Captain Rathke continued to be as defiant and proud as he was in life. Was the World War II soldier keeping an eye on him? It's something to consider. Rathke's use of the middle finger is also interesting. During World War II the practice was to hold up two fingers with the palm facing inward (a reverse of the peace sign), not to use the middle finger. However, Rathke was alive in the 1980s, when the middle finger was in more common use.

Rathke was not the only nefarious figure we met in the Meeting Room. At the height of our contact with the horde of angry male spirits, an MIB was sitting in a chair at the conference table. Later in the evening, one of the mediums on our team, Bryon, who did not know the lore about their Asian-like looks, drew him just that way.

Bryon Bartlett's sketch of the MIB he saw.

It is interesting to note that Jerry, whom we told you about in the chapter on Dr. Thompson's room, was playing cards with other spirits in the Meeting Room on a night soon after. As you will see in the next chapter, Jerry and the MIBs at the Webb have a mysterious connection.

We encountered quite a few transient spirits in the Meeting Room. Some of the random communications through the P-SB11 were "O'Connell," Where's ——?" "Gotta have it right," "Stewart," "A million dollars," and "Virgin."

We also met a spirit named Courtney who was with her "Granny," and a woman named Edna who said on the P-SB11 that she was "trying hard" to communicate. One night, Tonya saw a "little person" and heard the name "Jack."

On a quiet evening while the guests scanned the room with the equipment, Joey looked over his notes and thought about the next blog he and Tonya would write when "On Facebook" came across the P-SB11 (which is where we published our blog each week). Several months later, Tonya was telling people that they could go on the investigation's Facebook page to follow our progress, and a male spirit she saw standing behind Joey said, "Me, too."

As the guest investigators canvassed the Meeting Room on another night in the summer of 2017, we heard sounds we could not account for. We then heard a deep, echoing male voice say, "Bitch!" and "Fuck you!" Tonya replied, "We didn't call you names," to which he replied, "Bullshit!" Early on these were the types of things Vincent said toward the end of the night, shouting them from the doorway. But this was not Vincent. We hadn't heard from him for months. Apparently one of the angry male spirits was mimicking his behavior. On another night we heard a maniacal man's laugh come out of the P-SB11.

During that same difficult period, one corner of the Meeting Room was several degrees colder than anywhere else in the room. A guest remarked, "I feel like someone's watching me," to which a voice on the P-SB11 replied, "I'm gonna get ya" and "I'm watching." One evening, in response to the question, "Who is this now?" we heard, "A person."

Another night a female voice said on the P-SB11, "Leave." Joey asked if she wanted us to go and she said, "Just go!" We did.

On Halloween night 2017, as we returned from a second exploration of the Portal Hallway, the door to the Meeting Room, which had been wide open, was partially closed. It was a clear message that the spirits were not in the mood for any more visits.

Machinery was heard in the Meeting Room on several occasions, which might have been an "echo" of the former garment training facility. In late July 2016 a sensitive heard a man say, "Don't sit here" in reference to a bench against the wall. Tonya sensed a man in a leather apron. A week later he said, "Cleaning" in response to our question, "What are you doing?" Joey asked if he meant the textile machines. "Yes," he answered. One night a few weeks later he stood in the corner of the room moving his arm up and down, as though applying grease or painting. About a month later, he told us his name was James. Joey asked if he worked for or knew Vincent. Tonya and another sensitive got uneasy feelings. The sensitive got so dizzy and nauseated she had to crouch down on the floor. We closed the investigation for the night. We never encountered James again.

One night, a teenage guest reported a dream he had had almost a month before where he was in a blue room exactly like the Meeting Room. There was writing on the wall that said, "When you move, everything moves with you." He then heard, "You might need one of these," and saw a cross on the wall that rotated from an upright position to an inverted one.

A cross, inverted or otherwise, was not needed that night.

During the summer of 2017 a map of the Outer Banks in the Meeting Room near a row of cabinets stayed consistently mid-range on the EMF meters for weeks. Over time the area of electromagnetic activity widened by two feet. •

One evening in July, the temperature went up seven degrees in that area without an earthly explanation. We knew from experience that it might mean that the spirit of a burn victim was nearby. Soon after, we heard on the P-SB11, "I will ... everything is hot." A guest, who was a sensitive (we had four of them with us that night, none of whom we had met before), reported feeling her wrists were hot and felt tied down. Another sensitive coughed upon feeling a choking sensation and smelling soot. He further reported feeling a laceration on his chest (nothing physically manifested). Tonya felt that someone was in immense pain near the cabinets, or perhaps on the other side of the wall.

We heard on the P-SB11, "Jeffrey tell." (Weeks before we had heard on the spirit box, "Hello Jeff.")

One of the sensitives saw three spirits standing outside the door, watching us. He sensed that they wanted to help but didn't know how and were embarrassed. We heard the name "Minnie" on the P-SB11. We heard, "Medic here," "Yes," and "Correct." The spirits were asking us to do something with the notebook Joey used for field notes, but we did not know what. We asked for more information and heard on the P-SB11, "Not comprehending" and "Try another way." We were sure they were trying to direct us to previous field notes that could help, but we could not find anything.

Tonya and another sensitive felt strongly that the man in pain was on the other side of the wall from where the map of the Outer Banks was, so we went into the Portal Hallway. The spirit was there, in excruciating pain and strapped to a gurney (recall the sensitive who felt her wrists were tied down). Tonya told him it was just a memory and he did not have to be in pain any more. One of the sensitives thought, "Hold my hand if you need to" and felt the man's hand in his. Tonya asked everyone to pray or send white healing light for his peace. We did. All the sensitives felt him release and move on.

The next week, the map in the Meeting Room that shares the wall with where the man crossed over no longer lit up the EMF meters.

16
Open Up the Book
The Cannon Room

Although there were several provocative quotes we could have used for the title of this chapter, we chose "open up the book" because we often had experiences in this room connected to the books that line its shelves. The Cannon Room (so named because of its working replica cannon—which fired from compressed air, not gunpowder!) is the repository of the original volumes that Eva Webb and the Women's Club of Morehead City used to start the lending library. Many of them date back a hundred years or more. The room is filled with hundreds of other volumes as well, including many classics.

The spirits had a particular affinity for Ernest Hemingway. One night, impressions from sensitives indicated that the spirits wanted us to read a certain book. Joey asked the sensitives which one. One of the women replied, "*The Old Man and the Sea.*" She felt her hair touched. She stood up and a sweep of the EMF meter showed a spike to red. Tonya realized the guest had been "sitting on" John, who was a funny flirt with a love of music whom we discuss at length later in the chapter. Months before a guest had mentioned *The Old Man and the Sea* in the Meeting

The Cannon Room. John's corner is to the right of the cannon.

Room in connection with the spirit communications we were getting. A few days later the spirits asked a guest to look at a specific page in another Hemingway classic, *A Farewell to Arms*.

One night we were once more drawn to Hemingway. We thought it was again *A Farewell to Arms*. From the P-SB11 we heard, "Open up the book." A guest asked, "What page?" We thought we heard, "Two hundred sixty-eight." We heard, "Down" and "Upstairs, Downstairs." Another voice said, "It's a different one." We then got the correct Hemingway title: *For Whom the Bell Tolls*. The guests again asked for a page number. "Thirty-seven" was the answer. The following was read out loud from that page by a guest: "I don't believe in such things." One of the guests looked surprised and said, "I was just thinking 'I don't believe in ghosts.'"

A few nights later, as we were telling the guests about our experiences with Hemingway's books, Joey mistakenly said that it happened three times. A voice from the P-SB11 said, "Four." We checked our field notes and the voice was correct!

One night a sensitive was drawn to a book. She said it was red and said "Warner" on it. We found a multi-volume series of books matching that name and color. We were told by a spirit that the right book was volume 17. We asked for assistance in finding what they wanted. Two spirits came through the box saying, "October," "December," and "46," but they argued and one said, "Not that." The next night we tried to get more information about the book but were unsuccessful in getting coherent answers.

We had a guest one night who had been on a paranormal tour of the Webb four years earlier. She pointed to a shelf where she had reportedly gotten a welt from touching it. Right there was a book called *The Ethyl Corporation*. That morning Tonya had remarked to Joey that she wanted to do more Webb research. Before she and Joey had left for the Webb that night Joey researched Mr. Webb online because it never made sense that he was chief executive officer of General Motors, as some prior research had indicated. He was head of the Ethyl Corporation. The book was full of details about him and his family, some of which we shared in Chapter 3. We had unknowingly walked past that book dozens of times on prior visits.

In another synchronicity, in April 2017 a guest was pulled to page 369 of *Moby Dick*. It told of a carpenter and his wood shavings. Earlier that day, Joey had received an email from his friend Ishmael (named for the book's narrator), who had received a rare edition of the book for his fiftieth birthday. It is unclear what the page number/content meant.

One night Tonya was drawn to two books: *Gnomes* and *Jack*, which linked with the spirit she saw in the Meeting Room (mentioned in the previous chapter).

As our guests moved the EMF meters along the bookshelves one night in May 2017, two Agnes Turnbull books, *Nightingale* and *The Bishop's Mantle*, spiked the EMF meters to red. We asked if someone liked them and we heard, "I do" on the P-SB11. "Which do you like better?" we asked. The reply was, "Some of it."

Around this same time Tonya saw an older lady named Agnes in the Portal Hallway (early May) and in the Cannon Room (early June). We do not think that it was Agnes Turnbull, but it is a possibility. There was no more activity around the Turnbull books or the spirit named Agnes until a night in August when one of the guests from the May investigation returned and the Turnbull books again sent the EMF meter into red. The books continued to spike the EMF meters for the next several days.

Not long after we began our investigation of the Webb, Tonya saw what she described as a "cocky and arrogant" blond-haired male, dressed in modern yellow coveralls, standing by the window behind where the cannon sits, or seated in a nearby chair. She said that he was "snarling and aggressive" and fancied himself a ladies' man. A few months later a guest investigator said that the coveralls were fisherman's attire, which the man confirmed. Some months later he told us he had gone fishing and had caught some drum (a popular local fish).

Soon after, he introduced himself on the P-SB11 as John. (Note: unless stated otherwise, all communications from John came through the spirit box.) Whatever personality he was trying to display to us that first time was now gone, replaced by enthusiastic greetings, a flirtatious nature, and a clear love of music—especially Broadway show tunes.

It could be that John was initially emulating Vincent. Perhaps he was imitating him in a playful way that Tonya misinterpreted. Whatever the explanation, John became as consistently communicative and friendly as Dr. T and the source of many memorable experiences for our guests and us.

As evidenced in previous chapters, John did not confine himself to the Cannon Room, although that is where we normally found him. It was never long after we entered the room and Joey hung the P-SB11 in a certain spot on the bookshelves that we heard either a burst of music (typically a few piano chords) or one of John's signature greetings, "Hey guys," "What's up," "Wassup," or "How you doin'?"

For about the first year, John was able to move the pieces on the glass chess set in the Cannon Room. The first time he moved several pawns. When we asked if he would move them again, he said, "Not yet." A night soon after, pawns moved four times after we put them back in place, while two male voices on the P-SB11 had some fun telling us in mischievous voices, "Don't!" or "Don't do that." About a month later, the chess pieces were moved back to their starting position after Joey started a game with two pawns. A few nights later Joey asked, "Wanna play chess?" John answered, "Certainly."

One night we placed the P-SB11 near the chessboard where one of the guests had been moving the pieces. A voice said, "Checkmate."

On a night in mid-summer 2017 two guests started playing chess. A voice said, "Stop," "Put it back," and "Don't touch the board." Just after that a creepy child's squeal came out of the P-SB11 (we think this was the first cry for help from Rachel, whom you read about in earlier chapters) and the spirit box began emitting strange, inhuman sounds. We shut it off.

One evening not long after, Tonya saw a big man who pounded his fist on the chessboard, although it was unclear why.

A pair of guests who returned to the Webb a year or so after their initial visit that first summer showed us a photo of a spectral hand over the chessboard (we asked for a copy of the photo, but never received one). For the first time in many months, several pieces moved that night. Although no image of a hand was captured, Tonya took a series of pictures when we entered the room that show an expanding ball of light.

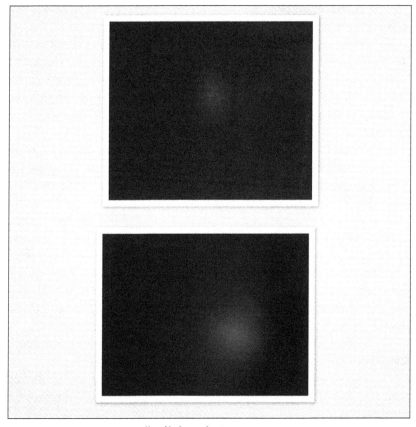

Balls of light in the Cannon Room.

151

One aspect of Tonya's initial feelings about John was consistent for a long time—John definitely fancied himself a ladies' man and loved to flirt (however, by the summer of 2017, around the time we were having the experiences with the angry male spirits, John stopped flirting with the guests).

One night in early summer 2016, John flirted with some of the female guests, asking, as they came near the spirit box, "What's up?" When one guest asked, "Are you flirting with us?" he asked, "You like that?" He then said, "Hey, girls" and "Right on" a few nights later. One night he wasn't talking. Joey told the guests that John normally flirted, prompting a female guest to say she guessed her and her friend weren't pretty enough. John said, "Nooooo" and "That's not it."

A few nights later he was so anxious to get to flirting he was out in front of the library. We heard, "Girls!" on the P-SB11.

John said, "Come here" one night when a female guest was in the corner where John felt closest to the girls with whom he wanted to flirt. She moved closer and asked if that was what he wanted, and he said, "Please." He played a larger than normal amount of music through the P-SB11. As we were leaving, he said, "Here's some more" and we heard piano music.

About a week later, John looked sad and confused. An intuitive felt drawn to the Hemingway title, *For Whom the Bell Tolls.* The guest felt there was information on page 313. Just before this, a female sensitive sat beside John, who was on the couch. He had told us he was there, and a temperature gun decreased five degrees and the EMF meters spiked only in the center of the couch where he sat. On page 313 was a passage about a sad man who was comforted by a girl, which was exactly what was happening! John also had two books on Henry VIII slightly pulled out from the shelves near where we always put the P-SB11 for him. Joey had talked about Henry VIII on his pirate tour the previous day (which, notably, is not a normal topic for the tour).

John sat on one of the couches one night in the Cannon Room staring at a spirit of a woman sitting on the opposite couch.

As we said, by summer of 2017 John was doing much less flirting with the girls (living or deceased), but one thing did not change—his great love of music.

One night, he said, "*Lay-*dees!" Joey asked if anyone knew the musical *Hamilton,* a Broadway hit that uses rap and hip-hop to tell the story of one of the most influential of America's "Founding Fathers." Hamilton is perhaps best known for dying in a duel with Aaron Burr.

Two teens answered, "Yes." John played a musical chord. Joey said that "*Lay*-dees!" sounded like a line from the song "Winter's Ball." John said, "Hamilton," "Girls," and "Ladies." He then asked all six girls on the tour to stand in his corner where the bookshelves came together in the back of the room. They did.

A few months later, Joey told John that he had been listening to *Hamilton* and John replied, "The king." Joey had indeed been listening to and singing the king's songs.

While Joey was setting up for the pirate educational program one night in April 2017, he sang Aaron Burr's song "Wait for It" from *Hamilton*. A few minutes later, as he passed Tonya in the front foyer on his way to the car for more props, she reached into a "free book" box and pulled out Gore Vidal's *Burr*. This synchronicity might be easily dismissed if it were not for the fact that John had had several exchanges with us about *Hamilton*.

One night in mid-summer 2017 John made a violin motion and said, "Songs." The music major with the group that night, whose focus was vocal training, sang a few verses of a song from the Broadway musical *Wicked*. John said, "Another." The singer asked if he wanted another song and John said, "Sure." John made a motion like he was wiping tears away with a handkerchief after the singer sang part of a sad song from *Les Miserables*. A female voice said, "Continue" and a male voice said, "Thank you." Our guest bowed and so did John.

John asked one night if we could play some music. We played some show tunes on a smartphone.

He sat in a chair next to Joey one evening, which was a first. He showed Joey smoking a pipe (a pastime Joey enjoys) and in a taxicab in New York to Tonya, which she saw as a series of short movies in her mind's eye. (A few weeks later, Joey's son invited him to New York City, where he lives, to see some Broadway shows.) He also mimed playing a fiddle. We had listened to Charlie Daniels' "Devil Went Down to Georgia" on the drive to the Webb.

One night after hearing the piano chords on the P-SB11, a guest asked if John liked music, and he said, "Yes."

A few weeks later, we had a guest from Long Island, New York. John was eager to "meet" him—he motioned toward the guest as we entered the room. The guest asked him if he was from New York and John said "Oh, yeah!" Outside, before the investigation started, the guest told us he didn't like the city and only went there a few times a year for sporting events and Broadway musicals. We found out later that his father was a musical theater performer. No wonder John wanted to meet him.

In early September 2017 John was talkative. One night Joey was telling the guests about how John used to flirt and once had six pretty young ladies crammed into his corner. John exclaimed, "Whoo!"

By the end of 2017, John focused more on Joey and Tonya directly, saying hello to them by name (he said the names of a few other guests as well). Tonya asked him one night what was happening, and he replied, "Nothin."

John served as a meter for what was happening upstairs. One night when the angry spirits were active he was out in the hall, saying things like, "Don't know why" and "I don't know," as if he was just as confused about things as we were. Something was keeping him from being in the Cannon Room. On nights when things were at their most difficult, John was not in the room.

In early February 2018 John's two great loves—music and girls—came together. We heard John's music as soon as we entered the room. He was in his corner, holding a violin—a new development (prior to that he only mimed a violin). He played it and everyone in the group (eight people) heard the violin coming from the P-SB11. Tonya asked him if he was playing the violin in honor of Valentine's Day coming up and he nodded yes. He again played the violin for us in mid-April 2018.

As hip and modern as John was (the musical *Hamilton*, for instance, was only a few years old), there were some phrases and slang of which he was not aware. One night one of the guests said to him, "See ya, home slice" as the group was leaving. John asked, "What did you just call me?"

Besides John, we met several other friendly spirits in the Cannon Room. One night, several guests and both Joey and Tonya heard an old man's kind voice from the corner of the room. This was NOT through the P-SB11. A night soon after, a young guest in her early teens became increasingly psychic as the investigation went on. She saw a man with a bushy beard in one of the armchairs the same time Tonya did. They said he looked Irish.

A few nights later we found out the old man was named Adam. He liked to do scrimshaw. He dumped water out of his boots. Through a series of yes and no questions from Tonya and three guests Googling information to produce questions and verify answers, we learned he was killed when his fishing vessel capsized during the September 1944 Great Atlantic Hurricane, which did immense damage to the Outer Banks. He told us about the Coast Guard cutters *Jackson* and *Bedloe*, both of which sank in the storm, causing the deaths of 48 sailors. Perhaps not coincidentally, given the prominence of U-boat-related phenomena in this book, they were on their way to rescue a merchant ship called the *George Ade* that had been struck by a torpedo from a U-boat when they capsized.

Teenagers becoming aware of their innate psychic abilities in the Webb was not unusual. Tonya believes we all have these abilities and the Webb was active enough to make some people aware that they had them. A teenage guest in the Cannon Room sensed something was on the couch one night and then said it moved. An EMF meter was placed in the indicated spot and it spiked red.

Tonya saw three Mennonite men in the Cannon Room one night in the summer of 2017. Other sensitives had described men of similar appearance going back to the previous summer. A week later, Tonya and another sensitive saw a man wearing Mennonite clothing; two weeks later he was seen reading a Bible. Bryon, one of our guest mediums, saw and drew three of them standing together in early August 2017.

One evening, Tonya described one spirit as an older man with a "scraggly" beard. He responded through the P-SB11, "Why do you say that?" She was embarrassed for insulting him but gently replied that was how it looked. He did not respond.

As with most of the rooms in the Webb, there were also unfriendly spirits that we encountered in the Cannon Room. One night there was no activity. Joey was saying to the guests that it was an unusually quiet night [meaning for the spirits who normally communicate] when the deep, echoing male voice we mentioned in previous chapters did not let him finish. He said, "Bullshit!" At that point, Joey said, "We're gonna go," and a voice said, "Night." We said, "Goodnight" and a voice replied, "Helllllllooooo!" followed by another that said, "Go. Move on."

Later that week, in response to a guest asking if we should stay in the room, we heard on the P-SB11, "Leave." Another voice asked, "Who are you?" We again heard, "Leave." We did. Another night we asked if anyone was in the room and a female voice said, "You are."

In early September 2017 it was getting near 11 PM (we were running 15 minutes longer than usual). One of the guests asked if the spirits wanted us to leave. An angry male voice said, "YES!" We did. Just to make sure, the spirit completely killed the P-SB11 for three minutes. It would not switch on, although it worked fine once we got downstairs.

One night we finished a quiet investigation with a group of 20. Even John and Vincent were nowhere to be found. This was not surprising, for there was an inverse correlation between group size and amount of activity in the Webb. The larger the group, the less communication. This became such an issue that we asked the tour company to reduce the maximum group size to 15. After 60-plus public investigations and 15 other trips to the Webb we can say that the ideal group size was six to eight. On that particular night we had some fellow investigators staying with us who had traveled from the Midwest to experience the Webb, so we decided to take them back upstairs after everyone else had left. In the Cannon Room the EMF meters spiked red on every chair. Through the P-SB11 we heard a female voice say, "We have the room!" We respectfully left.

Another night we heard a woman's voice in distress come through the P-SB11 three times. We had heard a moaning woman several times through the spirit box in the Cannon Room on previous visits, going back more than half a year. We were not able to discern who she might be or what her story is about.

Guests reported the floor around the cannon vibrated, as though the compressor stored under the floor was on (it was not). Then, one evening, if anyone stood within an outline of a circle stained in a faded black substance near the replica cannon, they got sick to their stomach, Joey included. The circle was roughly 18 inches across. The next morning, Joey called several people who knew the library well and none of them could say what the circle was for. It never again produced that effect. That same night, a spirit in a 1940s-era blue suit was facing the wall, afraid. A few weeks later Jolie learned that the spirit's name was Jacob. The night she saw him, there were lots of other people around him, laughing, drinking, and playing charades. In early September 2017 Jacob was again in the Cannon Room and was relaxed. He winked at a guest medium.

During the height of the troubles with the angry male spirits, guests noticed some odd things about the portrait of Eva Webb in the Cannon Room. They said that it was "creepy" or "weird," which surprised us—she was an attractive young woman when the portrait was painted. The portrait spiked to red when the EMF meters were held to it. We thought that one of the dark spirits had attached itself to the portrait. By the fall it no longer registered on the EMF meters and guests were back to remarking on how elegant and pretty she was.

Before we left the Cannon Room one evening Joey asked, "Anyone want to tell us anything?" A voice on the P-SB11 replied, "Stupid."

Some of the random communications we received through the P-SB11 in the Cannon Room were, "It's a ghost town," "Looking at that," "Houston," "Kids," and "Car."

Even for the Webb, the Cannon Room was especially active. We received a report from a regular visitor to the library who had her dress touched and saw a book come off a shelf in front of her in 2016.

One of the oddest instances of physical phenomena we experienced in the Webb occurred the night that the burn victim on the gurney was crossed over (Chapter 15). A 1978 silver dollar appeared out of thin air, from the perspectives of Tonya and another guest, and rolled along the floor in front of Tonya and three guests.

The silver dollar that appeared out of the air in the Cannon Room.

Before we continue, we want to point out that it had been a long and difficult night. We had a drunken bachelorette party of eight middle-aged women with us most of the evening who were unruly, used the bathroom several times (one of them to be sick), and tended to wander off. So we were not thinking clearly when the silver dollar appeared and rolled along the floor. We had felt so bad for the other guests (four of whom were sensitives) that we offered to stay to continue the investigation after the bachelorette party left. That was when the burn victim was crossed over and the silver dollar appeared.

Tonya, thinking it was the right thing to do, let the woman who picked up the silver dollar, Sabrina E, keep it. As you will see from the excerpts from an email she sent us several weeks later (and is graciously letting us share), this was not the right decision for what was obviously, in hindsight, a haunted object.

Excerpts from Sabrina E's email

"One of my sisters and I participated in... your paranormal tour towards the end of July... we were with (but not part of) the middle-age bachelorette party... after [they] left we continued to investigate... a silver dollar randomly fell from the chair I was sitting in. ...We couldn't figure out where it had come from.

"After [Tonya] took some photos she told me that since I found it I could keep it. Once I returned home I explained to my husband the odd circumstances that led to us finding this coin. I placed it on our kitchen counter and soon forgot it was there. ... My husband and I own two Siberian huskies. ... My male (Axle) is protective of me. ...
"While [my sister who came on the tour] was here Axle was acting strange. I assumed it was due to the lack of attention he was receiving. He would lay in the corner of our dining room and whimper every evening. When it was time for bed he would refuse to go to the bedroom with us. He usually sleeps in our bed. After [my sister] left he finally started going to our bedroom to sleep again, but he continued to act strangely. He would wake me up in the middle of the night crying (he normally sleeps longer hours than I do). I would eventually give in and let him outside. Once he was out he would sit in the yard whimpering and throw a tantrum when I would try to get him back indoors. This continued for over a week.

"One night he stood on the floor beside the bed, put his front paws on me and pounced up and down until I got out of bed. The next night I was sleeping and was jolted awake by my ponytail being pulled violently. When I looked in the direction of where my hair was pulled nothing was there. I turned back around to find Axle sitting up in the bed, staring in that same direction, crying. I finally convinced him to lay down beside me that night, but he started to shake uncontrollably. No matter what I did he just continued to shake. After that week or so had passed Axle started to come to bed with us ... but would disappear in the middle of the night. He would wander into [a different sister's room] and wake her up. He was doing the same things with her as he was doing with me.

"Whimpering all night and shaking uncontrollably. That again lasted for about a week. Last week I was having a conversation with my husband and I mentioned to him that I was glad Axle had started acting normal again. That was when my husband told me that he got rid of the coin. I asked him what coin he was referring to because at this point I had completely forgotten about the silver dollar. He told me that Axle started acting weird the night I brought that coin home. My husband thought there was a link, so he had been moving the coin around the house. When [my sister who came on the tour] left our house he moved it to our bedroom. After I had so many nights without sleep he moved it to [my sister's] room. When the same things were occurring in her bedroom he decided he wanted it out of our home."

As we said, things are clearer in hindsight. To send a guest home with an object that had probable paranormal origins was a mistake. Although it was a long and difficult night we were responsible for what happened and are grateful that the disturbance to Sabrina and those in her household (including poor Axle!) was not worse.

We cannot help but wonder where the coin is (her husband brought it to the bank) and what the current holder of the silver dollar is experiencing. Sabrina returned to the Webb on Halloween night 2017. She reported that no more activity had occurred in her home after the coin was removed.

While the experience with the apported silver dollar certainly qualifies as "high strangeness," the series of encounters we have chosen to close this chapter may just top it.

During Memorial Day weekend 2017 we encountered what can best be described as classic Men in Black (MIBs), which most people

159

know through the popular films with Will Smith and Tommy Lee Jones. As fantastical as those films are, they do get some elements right. MIBs dress in all black and appear when someone has seen a UFO or extraterrestrial or interdimensional—especially if they plan to talk about what they have seen.

Tonya clairvoyantly saw two MIBs in the chairs by John's shelves. They were identical in appearance: black suits, pale skin, and they acted "robotic," as though they did not know how to behave as humans. They sat with their backs ramrod straight, hands on their knees. They looked like humorless government workers. To Tonya, they seemed to be more like projections than spirits. The MIBs jammed the P-SB11 to the point that it ceased to work, even with a new battery. It was clear they did not want us to communicate with any of the spirits present. Tonya tried to communicate with them telepathically, but they did not answer.

We saw a mysterious male spirit in several areas of the Webb who might also have been an MIB. He was described by various mediums and sensitives as "tall," "stern," and "gaunt." He was first seen in Dr. T's room in July 2016. Two weeks later he was in the hall leading to the Back Stacks. Twelve days later he was in the Meeting Room. Tonya referred to him as the "Undertaker." A few nights later Tonya referred to him as the "Undertaker" again and he said on the P-SB11, "I'm not." The adjectives listed above describe how many witnesses have perceived MIBs (as well as the Internet-born phenomenon, "Slenderman"). In one case in particular, a researcher was approached in 1980 by an MIB closely fitting this description. This encounter also happened in a library.

About a week after our first MIB encounter, two guests saw the spirit of a man in a black suit cross the first floor hallway. Tonya tried to get a picture. The facial recognition box activated on her phone and one of the staircase motion sensors went off near to where the spirit stood. The camera refused to focus and, after one of our guests stood where he had seen the spirit, there were just two streaks of light where the guest should be standing. This happened with three consecutive photos. We got a lot of deep-voiced male communications on the P-SB11 soon after, much of it random phrases or impossible to interpret. A spirit in a dark suit stood all night in the courtyard entrance, as if he were a guard. Based on his clothes, shoes, and the way he stood, we believe it was also an MIB.

On July 5, an MIB was again at the courtyard door. When we entered the Cannon Room near the end of the night's investigation, two MIBs were waiting for us, standing this time. Only Tonya could see them. Jerry, the African American gambler, once again acting as Tonya's self-appointed protector (see Chapter 13), said, through the P-SB11, "(In?)competent" and "Guessing." The MIBs tried to keep Jerry from communicating with us by closing his throat. He looked so frightened and distressed that Tonya summoned angel energy to rescue him. The MIBs jammed the P-SB11, just like they did during our previous encounter. Tonya saw an MIB standing with his hands out in a blocking motion in front of the kitchen door.

First floor hallway ending with the courtyard entrance.

The next morning, we received a message from one of the guests who was with us that night. He had had a dream in which John came to him and said he was kept quiet, not by the MIBs, but by the hairy, clawed interdimensional we first encountered near the kitchen (see Chapter 13). Vincent was kept quiet by it too. Did Vincent stop communicating because of the MIBs and the interdimensional? The timing of his disappearance and our encounters with them line up almost to the day. It is also a possibility that the angry male spirits were drawn in by the energy of the interdimensional. This is all speculation, but the timeframes are too close to ignore.

Eight days after the attack on Jerry by the MIBs, according to the National UFO Report Center (NUFORC) Database, on July 13, 2017 at 9 PM, a man living on the nearby Bogue Sound and his father saw a large UFO pass over Morehead City. They had experience with aircraft and went so far as to call the nearby Cherry Point Air Station and Camp Lejeune to confirm that no military craft were in the area at that time. They even checked satellite records and found nothing.

UFOs were also reported over Morehead City (some in near proximity to the Webb) to MUFON in March 2010, and May and August 2012, and to NUFORC in June 1955, January 2003, April 2014, and December 2015. In most of these reports, like the one in 2017, the residents were familiar with military aircraft because of their proximity to Cherry Point Air Station and they were confident they saw UFOs.

Several weeks later, MIBs returned to the Cannon Room. This is interesting because, earlier in the day, Joey talked with someone about the MIBs and their attack on Jerry. To add to the mystery, we had received an email earlier that day from someone who wanted to send us a photo she took of the hairy interdimensional whose appearance coincided with the first appearance of the MIBs. Were Joey's talking about them and the offer of the photo (which we never received) the reason why the MIBs appeared that night? Did the MIBs interfere in some way with our receiving promised photos? As you have read in these pages, we had at least half a dozen instances where photographers agreed to send us photos but they never arrived.

As we wrapped up the investigation, Tonya said that no one had found a Bigfoot. A voice from the P-SB11 said, "I did." Perhaps the MIBs had finally decided to speak.

17
Ten-Four

Contact with Deceased Family and Friends

It was never our intention to hold séances or otherwise contact specific deceased individuals during our investigations in the Webb, and we held true to that plan over the course of our two-year investigation. What we did not anticipate was that deceased individuals would come to the Webb without prompting in order to communicate with their living family members and friends. It should be mentioned that, during this two-year period, Tonya had more visits from the dying or deceased as her abilities as a medium increased. The implications of these visits as far as the nature of life after death and of space–time are considerable. As you will see, there were instances where the deceased family member arrived at the Webb the first time weeks *before* the people to whom they were connected. The details related during these communications make a strong case for life after death and the fact that our loved ones are at times interested in what is going on in our lives after they die.

In the middle of July 2016 we had two consecutive nights when members of our guest investigation teams were contacted by a deceased member of their family.

The first night, a three-generation family came to the Webb, hoping to talk to their deceased patriarch. They had not made this intention known prior to their arrival, nor for the first half of the investigation. The youngest of the group, a 13-year-old boy celebrating his birthday, told Joey why they'd come as the two of them were investigating the area behind the kitchen while the rest of the group was in the hallway. Joey wanted to say something to Tonya about the family's hopes but he didn't get the chance.

Later in the evening, while we were in the Meeting Room, the boy was sitting on one of the couches. He turned the EMF meter toward his chest. It spiked to red and stayed there for several minutes. This was a new experience for us. As everyone watched in amazement they wondered aloud, "Is it grandpa/dad?" At that moment Joey heard a name in his mind, repeated over and over. Since he had never had a clairaudient experience, he initially dismissed it, but when the repetition of the name grew more insistent, he finally asked the family if the name meant anything to them. It was the deceased patriarch's name. As they acknowledged this, he came through the P-SB11. They had a short but moving conversation with him, including a little humor as he spoke the name of another member of the group who had distanced himself from the experience the entire night— the man was the widow's new boyfriend! The look on the man's face as his name was spoken is something we will never forget. The deceased husband/father/grandfather ended the communication with "Ten-four" when we let him know we were leaving, something his daughter-in-law told us he often said.

The following night, a previous visitor to the Webb came back and brought her mother, who was contacted by her husband, who had been deceased for 12 years.

Our third experience with contact from a deceased family member occurred in the hallway by the Intro Room on a night in late July 2017. We encountered a man six feet five inches tall with broad shoulders who greeted us with a friendly laugh. He then said, "Ten-four" through the spirit box. Through clairaudience, Tonya got the name "George." One of the guests had a deceased father with that name. He was a police officer. "Ten-four" was something he often said. Of note, we had heard his laugh and "Ten-four" two weeks earlier on the P-SB11 in the same spot without seeing him. This is strong evidence that the deceased police officer was first at the Webb *six weeks before* his daughter and widow arrived at the library.

The coincidence of our being contacted by two deceased men who used "Ten-four" while communicating with their families almost exactly a year apart is also too rich to ignore.

About a month later a group of guests asked if they could contact their deceased uncle. Tonya asked them to focus on him. She soon saw and described a man in red suspenders, with white hair and a big smile; it was their uncle. He lectured them about driving too fast (something Dr. T had done earlier in the evening). They said that the uncle "freaked out" about it all the time. Was Dr. T anticipating the visit that was to come?

Bryon, the medium who worked with us on occasion after being trained by Tonya, received a message one night for her and Jolie that consisted of the words and phrases "Starseed," "Star child," and "Indigo." Although these words might seem meaningless to someone else, they were profoundly connected to Tonya and our daughter, and have been since Jolie was two. Bryon also had a message for Joey: a pinky ring and the Italian word *Reficio*. Joey knew this was a message from his paternal grandfather, whose pinky ring he inherited. *Reficio* means to "make over, make anew; remake, restore, repair." This had a clear and timely meaning for Joey.

In the Meeting Room one night a frequent guest who spent a lot of time in the library felt someone touch her back and hair. After a few communications from the P-SB11 and some of Tonya's observations she knew it was her deceased grandfather, about whom she had been thinking after seeing the film *Dunkirk*.

A few days later we got transmissions in the Meeting Room from the P-SB11 from a male voice saying, "Hall," "Present," and "Sunday." Based on these communications, one of the guests thought it might be her biological father. Tonya saw a man in a brown suit at the end of the conference table, presenting white flowers. (A picture that a guest took showed a band of light at the end of the table.) "What is your question?" was asked of the guest who thought it was her biological father. We heard, "Do you do that?" which no one understood.

We heard a name, which we are changing to "Nicky" to keep the family anonymous, followed by "Time." The family realized that the person coming through the P-SB11 was a family member whose ashes they had scattered the night before at the beach a town over from the Webb. We moved to the Cannon Room, and Nicky said, "It's a metaphor" and "[unintelligible] house." One of the guests looked up white flowers online and found they symbolize "the glittering waves off a sandy beach," which described the scene of the previous night in perfect detail. Nicky said, "Clarissa [a pseudonym for one of the guests], I am with you."

It is difficult to describe how much this meant to the family, who had made a long trip to scatter Nicky's ashes near a place he loved. His traveling across time and space to acknowledge their effort meant the world to them.

There was an angry male spirit wearing a hat standing in the Meeting Room one night. A guest heard the man's name through the P-SB11 and also some discussion Joey and Tonya had about this spirit, whom they had encountered several times in prior weeks. The guest expressed to Joey that perhaps it was the guest's deceased father, whose name was the same as the spirit's. Some of the P-SB11 responses that Joey received both in the parking lot before the investigation started and during the night pointed to this possibility. They correlated with facts about the guest's deceased father, but they were not conclusive, and we were careful to not communicate to the guest that this was definitely her father.

If it was this girl's father, this is another instance where the spirit showed up in the Webb well in advance of the guest to whom he was attached.

That same night, the grandmother of one of the guests showed up. She was meticulous, without a hair out of place, and to the point, gesturing and saying things to Tonya that made it clear who she was for the guest.

On a night in late August 2017 we had an entomologist on the investigation. He asked many questions about life after death from a scientific point of view. About half an hour into the investigation he asked if people can talk to those who have crossed over. Tonya said that it happened in the Webb on occasion. He told us the name of a close friend in his early twenties who had recently died of heart complications. Tonya saw his friend standing next to him. Another medium saw him as well.

The spirit said through the P-SB11, "Dude, what's up?" We were in the Children's Room, which made sense to the guest because his friend loved kids. We went upstairs. While we were in the Portal Hallway, the guest asked his friend what he thought about all the spirits surrounding him. Tonya said he did a "no good" motion with his hand. He then said on the P-SB11, "Duuude."

In the Intro Room at the end of the night, the guest asked his deceased friend if he should worry about, look into, or research life after death. From the P-SB11 we heard, "No, sir." The guest asked if he should concentrate on studying and teaching. "Yes" was the answer. Tonya saw rubber-soled canvas shoes and a shoebox. She sensed that the deceased friend was saying that his friend would have proof of life after death tied to these items in the future.

In Chapter 9 we reported that on Halloween 2017 we watched the creases on two chairs in the Back Stacks change shape, as if someone was sitting and moving around in them. The second spirit that communicated with us through the P-SB11 said the name "Lindsey" [a pseudonym] who was the guest closest to the chair. Lindsey asked, "Are you family?" to which the spirit replied, "Probably." He said, "It's my favorite," and Lindsey realized that it was her father, who used to call her that. She was wearing his ashes around her neck. He said, "It's nice."

As a medium, Tonya has helped dozens of people communicate with their deceased relatives (Lindsey's father has been a persistent guest at readings Tonya subsequently did for her). For those who have never had such an experience, it is an emotional and often life-changing event, and the nights that this happened in the Webb are among our most memorable.

The frequency of these experiences in the Meeting Room, sharing as it does a wall with the Portal Hallway, makes perfect sense. The instances of spirits appearing at the Webb weeks before their family members arrived prompt big questions about the nature of space–time, quantum physics, and the parameters of reality as we perceive it.

In the final two chapters, we will examine what all this means for the field of paranormal investigation and our relationship with spirits and other beings beyond the veil.

18
It's a Ghost Town
Why is the Webb So Active?

Two years. Seventy-plus nights. More than 150 hours.

In that considerable amount of time the Webb was rarely quiet. Although the spirits made us earn their trust—the activity and interactions increased steadily as the months and investigations added up—it was without a doubt the most paranormally active site we have yet encountered, both in terms of quantity of spirits and phenomena and the broad spectrum of types.

In this chapter, we discuss the reasons why we think this is so.

Location

Many researchers (ourselves included) believe that geography plays a big role in the paranormal phenomena experienced in a specific location. Coming full circle, we immediately think of the sleepy West Virginia town of Point Pleasant, located at the convergence of the Kanawha and Ohio Rivers.

From November 1966 through December 1967 this quiet, peaceful town of 6,500 was plagued by strange visitors, including the so-called Mothman and the mysterious Men in Black, and unexplained events, which culminated in the tragic collapse of the Silver Bridge and the loss of 46 lives.

Some locals believe a curse on the land is responsible for the many strange sightings and tragic events in the area. Supposedly the curse was made by Shawnee Chief Cornstalk when he was shot to death by colonial soldiers in 1777. This theory has been all but debunked—it was most likely generated by a stage play from the early twentieth century. The historical record indicates that Cornstalk was shot before he had a chance to say anything at all. Rather, most of us remain convinced that it is the energetic influence created by the confluence of the Kanawha and Ohio rivers driving the phenomena. Strange lights and UFOs have been reported along these two rivers for decades and the supernatural lore of the local Indian tribes is abundant. Large areas of West Virginia were used only for hunting and not settlement because they were said to be inhabited by dark spirits.

Does much of this sound familiar? Many of the phenomena just described were also a part of our experiences at the Webb—including UFOs and MIBs! We even met our own Mothman-type figure at the Webb in the form of the clawed and hairy interdimensional.

It gets stranger. Morehead City is also at the confluence of two bodies of water: the Bogue Sound and the Newport River, which come together to form Beaufort Harbor. Proximity to salt water means abundant negative ions in the air—which make for excellent energy conductivity.

Beaufort Harbor is near to where the infamous Blackbeard scuttled his flagship, *The Queen Anne's Revenge*, in November 1718. There were rumors that his ghost was seen at the Webb, but we never encountered him, nor had anyone we interviewed. In another parallel, Blackbeard is the area's own version of Mothman—a larger-than-life figure that boosts a small town's economy by drawing tens of thousands of interested people year after year.

The communication from the P-SB11 that we chose for this chapter, "It's a ghost town," is not quite accurate—it is really a ghost *county*. Carteret County has more than a few haunted graveyards (the Old Burial Ground in Beaufort is the oldest public one in the state, dating to 1736, and we had many encounters with spirits there). Walking the waterfront in either Morehead City or Beaufort is almost sure to lead to a ghostly encounter at some point on the journey. All along the Bogue Sound are stories of hauntings attached to maritime and other tragedies. The deceptively named Crystal Coast has a darker moniker: the "Graveyard of the Atlantic." Going back to the 1500s, there have been over 5,000 vessels claimed by its treacherous waters—including the 300-plus sunk during World War II by German U-boats.

Given our multiple encounters in the Webb with sailors and others whose lives were woven with the sea, it is clear that location plays a big part in why the Webb is so active.

The Radio Tower

Just across Ninth Street is a powerful radio tower. The electromagnetic energy put out by the tower no doubt contributes to the near-perfect conditions for peak paranormal activity, not just in and around the Webb but perhaps the entire block. At a presentation we did for a book club in September 2017, one of the women in attendance showed us a photo she had taken outside the Methodist Church across the street from the Webb. It showed a cross of light radiating from the brickwork that could not be explained. As we were finishing this book, we met a woman who had worked at the former nursing home across Evans Street. She and another woman (independent of each other) both quit after working the third shift. The ceaseless sound of phantom slippered feet walking up and down the hallways night after night was more than they could take. Having met half a dozen or more of the deceased residents from the nursing home in the Webb, we know these women's experiences were not the result of middle-of-the-night overactive imaginations.

A Memorial to the Dead

Renovated, reinvented, and renamed in 1936 after the premature death of Earle Webb Jr., the library is literally a memorial to the dead. Although we never encountered Earle Jr. (or any of the Webbs) during our investigations, Earle Jr.'s portrait in the front foyer, looking like a character from an F. Scott Fitzgerald novel, is a sobering reminder of a young, promising life cut short, and the reason why the Webb building became the *Memorial* Library and Civic Center.

Two Doctors' Offices and a Burn Ward

Linked to the Webb being a memorial to the dead is the fact that it served as the space for two doctors' offices in its first incarnation and occasionally during World War II as a makeshift burn ward and triage for men injured when oil tankers were attacked by German U-boats and the hospital's resources were overwhelmed. With Dr. Royal's strong connection to the property across the street where the hospital used to sit and Dr. T's frequent residency in the Webb long after his death, it is clear that sickness, dying, and death have made a powerful, lasting impact on the rooms and hallways of the Webb.

Old Books, Furniture, and Objects

The Webb is filled with antique furniture, hundreds of books more than a century old, and display items that date back decades. The staff brings in new displays almost every month, from vintage hats to old works of art, which may attract or bring spirits with them. It could be that the high number of transient spirits we encountered in the Webb was due in part to these ever-changing displays that the staff brought in and out, depending on the season, upcoming holiday, or special program.

The Upstairs Hallway is Almost Certainly a Portal

As we discussed in prior chapters, the two windows facing each other at the ends of the long hallway upstairs have almost surely created a portal. The feeling of being in a vortex, or the dimensions of the Portal Hallway shifting before one's eyes or appearing separate and distinct, coupled with the appearance of the interdimensional and the skeletal creature on the ceiling all strengthen this hypothesis. The "Grand Central Station" feeling of the Portal Hallway—where spirits were seen in large numbers, voices overlapped, communications were the most random, and the EMF meters spiked to red near the ceiling and along the floor—is also evidence of a portal. It is also silly to discount the fact that several spirits told us on the P-SB11, "It's a portal."

The "Mothman Effect"

Of all the reasons why the Webb Memorial Library and Civic Center may be so active, we have saved perhaps the simplest for last. The Webb is well known for its activity. There were several prior incarnations of the ongoing investigation going back many years and paranormal groups from far and wide visited the Webb. During our two years there, we had guest investigators come from thousands of miles away to explore its haunted rooms. A notable percentage of those guests had either been aware of their mediumistic or sensitive abilities or were taken by surprise by what they suddenly were able to see or hear while they were there. We had several mediums become overwhelmed or request more training before they returned. As you read in these pages, the spirits were often happy to be seen and to interact with visitors—until they were not.

In the film *The Mothman Prophecies*, the lead character, a reporter named John Klein, goes to see a reluctant sensitive named Alexander Leek (take Klein's first name and reverse Alexander's last name and you get John Keel—the investigator who did more than anyone in the field to make Mothman and the UFO/MIB flap in Point Pleasant famous). He asks Leek, whose life has been shattered by his premonitions and visions, why it is now happening to him? Leek cocks his head, looks into Klein's eyes, and says, "You noticed them, and they noticed that you noticed them."

We call this the "Mothman Effect." For many years, people have noticed the spirits in the Webb and it is abundantly clear that they have certainly noticed us.

19
Get the Information Out There

What We've Learned and How it Applies to Paranormal Investigation Beyond the Webb

The opportunity to spend more than 150 hours doing a two-year investigation of such an active location as the Webb is a rare gift for a paranormal researcher, and we tried to make the most of it. In this chapter we offer a checklist of the practices and specialized knowledge that served us well in our investigations at the Webb and elsewhere. It is our hope that these methods will be useful to other paranormal researchers and help to move the field forward toward the legitimacy it has come to deserve.

Develop Your Intuition

The last thing Tonya told our guest investigators as we prepped them for an evening's investigation was "trust your intuition." We believe it is one of the most important skills that an investigator can possess. But what does this phrase mean and how does it apply to the field of paranormal investigating?

While this is a subject that deserves a book of its own (which Tonya has written, titled *Living the Intuitive Life: Cultivating Extraordinary Awareness*; it is full of exercises and strategies for developing your intuition), we can suggest some simple strategies here to get you started.

Meditation and deep breathing to quiet the mind and open the body's sensing systems are important. Our logical minds are designed to quickly pull stored data from the brain's memory systems when we are in an unfamiliar situation to help us make sense of things. Using meditation and breathing will slow that process down and allow you the opportunity to spend time with the unfamiliar rather than dismissing it as pure imagination or letting it frighten you away.

A developed intuition will also help with receiving and deciphering messages that the spirits share—both verbal and symbolic. Intuitive information is first received through the subconscious mind and the language of the subconscious is the language of symbols. Becoming familiar with symbols and archetypes will go a long way toward helping you to interpret the information and communications you receive during your investigations. We suggest starting with the work of Carl Jung.

Trusting yourself to be open and nonjudgmental as the messages and communications come through allows you to honor the spirits and make the most of what they are sharing.

A strong intuition is important for keeping your investigations safe. There are several instances in this book where intuition allowed us to see that what was happening on the surface was not the entire picture. Vincent immediately comes to mind. Intuition comes into play when deciding how far to go in an investigation. The need to know (and Joey readily admits that his is strong) sometimes leads you to ignore your intuition about what's best. The stronger your intuition is, the less likely you will dismiss it, or let your baser instincts override it.

Developing intuition is a discipline that takes constant practice. As developed as Tonya's intuition is, on a night when we were tired and so much was happening—both paranormally and otherwise—she allowed her desire to be generous and let someone go home with an object that was haunted override her intuition about the nature of objects that appear out of thin air. In such an active place as the Webb, all your skills—intuition included—will be tested time and again.

176

Protect Yourself Psychically

Given everything we said about intuition, once your sensing systems are open and your conscious control mechanisms somewhat suppressed, it is important to protect yourself psychically. As we reported, spirits followed us and some of our guests home, and we saw physical evidence of contact by spirits on the skin of some of our investigators. Others, Joey included, were touched or shoved.

The phenomena of spirits coming to and going from the Webb and interacting with guests and investigators either before or after a night of investigation were complicated. After a very active night of investigation, Joey had a lucid dream where he left his body and found himself in a dark, unidentified space. He homed in on a steady tone and realized it was the Walk/Don't Walk sign outside the Webb. Once he knew where he had been transported to, he went back into his body. The spirits were apparently not done interacting with him that night and had lured him back.

One night we had a spirit show up who had been attached to a guest when she was a child. It had been decades since the guest had communicated with this spirit, whom she called "the Major." He was an army officer from the northern United States who had fought in Mexico during the time of the infamous Mexican revolutionary Pancho Villa in the second decade of the twentieth century. The spirit named Josh that we communicated with in the summer of 2016, whom several sensitives recognized by his overalls, said to the Major, in his familiar Southern drawl, "We don't want your Yankee ghost down here!"

No one wants to be caught in the middle of a deep-rooted spirit-feud like that without the proper protection!

When you are psychically protected it is easier to establish boundaries with those spirits who like to touch people or otherwise try to invade their psychic space. Just as you would with a living person, a firm "Please don't touch me" or "Please don't be so close to me" will often do the trick, especially if you took the time to protect yourself with white light.

Before entering an active site, take several deep cleansing breaths, call upon your angels or guides for protection, and envision a circle of white light around you. Check in during the investigation with your guides and keep that circle of light going strong.

After investigating on active nights, we showered or bathed with Epsom salts, burned sage, and used feathers or other shamanic tools to clear our energy fields. A night of bad dreams or bringing home a mischievous spirit who knocks things over or otherwise makes life difficult for you is a sure reminder to take the time to protect yourself before, during, and after an investigation.

Do Your Research

One of the surest ways to help bring legitimacy to the field of paranormal investigation is to gather as many facts as you can about the location you are investigating (both in terms of geography and history) and about the people associated with it. As we have demonstrated throughout this book, research into the who, where, what, and when creates context that helps to make sense of the spirit communications and the types of spirits encountered. The more research-based context you have, the more likely it will be that these spirit activities and communications will make sense according to the rules and expectations of most people.

Scientists scoff at almost anything paranormal because they cannot measure and quantify it using accepted Scientific Methodology. But if they were to accept that there are other types of corroborative data besides weights and measures there would be less shaming and dismissal of people's experiences with the paranormal and humankind would benefit by expanding our concepts of everything from life after death, to how time functions, to the fact that, to quote Shakespeare's Hamlet, "There are more things in heaven and earth, Horatio, than are dreamt of in your philosophy." Subjective paranormal experience *can be* corroborated, and thus validated and given credence by history, geography, and the similar experiences of others, which means it's our responsibility as paranormal researchers to do our research—as mundane and tedious as it may be—to bridge the gap between the open-minded and the Horatios of the world.

As we demonstrated time and again in the preceding chapters, the land deeds, newspaper articles, nonfiction books, historical collections, and interviews that we collected by visiting courthouses, historical societies, cemeteries, and online databases such as MUFON contributed to substantiating and making sense of the encounters we had with spirits and other entities. This research was essential to the rigorous investigation that came with what we termed "CAP" (conditional anomalous phenomena). The satisfaction one gets from finding a piece of hard data—such as the declassified US Naval Command report that offered insight and corroboration into what we encountered with German U-boat captain Hellmut Rathke—makes all the miles, hours, and at times dead ends worth it. Although we can never truly remove the C from CAP, we can make the label of "conditional" much smaller by applying the hard data of research to a possible paranormal event.

There are many in the field of paranormal research who make a case for clear interconnections between hauntings, UFOs, cryptids (both flesh-and-blood and interdimensional), and the history of an area. The cross-disciplinary research we did connected with the Webb allowed us to present our own evidence for these connections in the pages of this book.

Have a Basic Understanding of Story

When he's not investigating the paranormal, Joey is a professional storyteller and content creator who writes, directs, and acts in a wide array of media. He also teaches creative writing and storytelling. As you've seen in this book, those skills are valuable when you have multiple encounters with a spirit over a long period of time or are trying to puzzle out what is going on at a haunted site or in the midst of a paranormal experience.

Space does not permit us to go into detail. Instead, we briefly discuss what Joey calls the "3 Threes of Good Storytelling." First, every story has a *Beginning*, *Middle*, and *End*. As paranormal researchers, we usually find ourselves at the *end* of the story (the circumstances of the spirit's death) or somewhere in the middle, which is the hardest part of a story to track because of its complexity. Research can often help us understand the beginning of the story. The more pieces of the puzzle, the easier it is to track what writers call the "arc": the movement from beginning to end, including any changes in personality and motivation (consider Vincent). Second, there is the *Who* (the characters), *Where* (the place), and *What* (the main problem). If you go back to Vincent or Hellmut Rathke, you can see the Who, Where, and What of their stories. In the realm of the living, the chapter on the history of the Webb has all these elements.

Third, there are the *Conflict*, *Climax*, and *Circumstances*. Our experiences in the summer of 2017 had plenty of conflict. So do the stories of Vincent, Hellmut Rathke, and Rachel. Rarely do we have a clear climax, although the stories in this book where spirits were crossed over by Tonya (alone or with other sensitives and mediums) certainly do. Circumstances are the most important aspect of storytelling to keep in mind when doing paranormal investigating. Joey explains Circumstances as how the Where and the What affect the behavior of the Who. Almost every story in this book, whether it is our experience, an experience of our guests, the spirits, or some combination thereof, has clear circumstances. A spirit such as Hugh who hid behind the couch in the Children's Room found his circumstances changed when Tonya could see him. His "Oh God!" was a clear indication of that.

The fundamentals of storytelling also help to make the paranormal accessible to a diverse group of people. One of Joey's living history colleagues says, "Go to where they are and bring them back with you." We've outlined in Chapter 2 how we did this with our guests. Although it is not our intention to convince anyone of anything—not our guests and not the readers of this book—we do try to thin the barriers of doubt enough to allow guests to feel open to possible experience.

An understanding of story allows the paranormal investigator to understand *tropes* (metaphorical use of words or expressions), *genre* (the recurring elements in a story type; Gothic horror is perhaps the best known, with its thunderstorms, cobwebby castles, and haunted forests), and *stereotypes* (repetitive, generalized traits). Many of our guests at the Webb came with high expectations. Everyone wanted to *see* a ghost, because characters can see them in the movies. As we said in Chapter 2, some guests wanted to bully the spirits to make them angry so that they moved things or slammed doors or cursed at us— because they saw that behavior on many of the paranormal "reality" shows. If we could dispel misinformation and misrepresentation in our introduction, there was a better chance that potential experiencers would be open to larger possibilities than what they were told all their lives about hauntings and ghosts.

Everyone remembers the villain in a story. They are often the most iconic characters, like Darth Vader and Dracula. So it's no surprise that oftentimes investigators focus on the tragedy, pain, and evil that encountered spirits represent. But most of the spirits we met in the Webb were benevolent and many of them enjoyed sharing their wisdom with us through their wit. Some spirits had boundary issues (*a form of over-*

enthusiasm from the other side), but a gentle request that they not touch the guests usually did the trick. This is another reason why we are always clear that few if any of the entities we encountered in the Webb were "demons," although many guests were quick to assume that about any dark or angry spirit. We can thank the "reality" shows for that as well.

Have a Working Knowledge of Quantum Physics

Throughout this book, especially in the chapters about the Portal Hallway and Communications from Deceased Relatives and Friends, we presented evidence that spirits appeared at the Webb before the people they were connected to showed up. This phenomenon can best be understood through the lens of quantum physics, as can the basic idea that spirits and interdimensionals can reside in a parallel universe a hair's-width away from our own.

Quantum physics serves as a nexus between Science and Spirit. In *A Brief History of Time* Stephen Hawking explored the theory that effects precede causes. Zen master Shunryu Suzuki quoted the founder of the Soto school, Dogen-zenji, in *Zen Mind, Beginner's Mind*, as saying, "Time goes from present to past." William Douglas Horden, a diviner and I Ching master who had the opportunity to visit the Webb early on in our investigation, writes in *Way of the Diviner*, "Because there exist no barriers between past, present or future in the *oneness of time*, the future creates the past as much as the past creates the future." From the Kabbalist tradition, we learned that "Quantum physics teaches us that the universe is not a collection of separate things moving in empty space. All matter exists in a great quantum web of connection."

A few of the principles of quantum physics that came into play most often in the Webb and apply in general to the field of paranormal research are *quantum entanglement* (i.e., *nonlocality*—the theory that particles far apart react instantaneously to movement by a counterpart) and the *Heisenberg Uncertainty Principle*, which postulates that the observer affects the observed. It is a good bet that this is why it is so difficult to collect hard, scientifically measurable data about the paranormal. To go back to the Leek quote that ends the previous chapter, not only are they "noticing that we notice"—spirits and other entities have the ability to shut down equipment, play with our perception (the ghost pretending to be a clown), and employ sarcasm and deceit when questioned. We believe that replication of phenomena is also difficult for these same reasons (see the later subsection "Test what you can"). Considered from a phenomenological point of view, David Abram, in explaining the work of Maurice Merleau-Ponty, wrote in *The Spell of the Sensuous*, "The event of perception, experimentally considered, is an inherently interactive, participatory event; a reciprocal interplay between the perceiver and the perceived." Many of the communications from the Webb's spirits demonstrated this complex interplay beyond a doubt.

Use Synchronicity Wisely

Synchronicity is often referred to as a "meaningful coincidence." Carl Jung, who coined the term, defined it as an "acausal connecting principle." It is easy to get carried away in applying synchronicity to paranormal events. As conscious as we are about synchronicities in our life (Joey keeps a detailed database of them going back more than 10 years), prior to this chapter we referred to synchronicity only 11 times and made an effort to provide context as to why we think each synchronicity is relevant to our investigation of the Webb. It can be a useful tool in moderation, especially with an understanding of quantum physics to undergird it; however, looking at every occurrence through the lens of synchronicity just muddies the investigative waters—and they are muddy enough already.

Don't Rely Solely on Technology

Another trend in the field—again driven by the "reality" shows—is the over-reliance on technology. After about a year at the Webb, we were contacted by someone whose mother, also a paranormal researcher, was no longer able to go on investigations. She wanted to donate her equipment to us. We gratefully accepted. The next several nights we brought several 3-in-1 devices, "ghost pumps," and alternative temperature gauges and EMF meters to the Webb. Within a week we put them all in storage and went back to our K2 meters, temperature guns, and the P-SB11.

As "ooh" and "aah" as some of these complicated devices are with their arrays of multi-colored lights, antennae, and toggle switches and knobs, they did not help us in any measurable way to communicate more efficiently or more often with the spirits. The fact is, oftentimes the EMF meters would spike to red but there were no temperature changes or communications on the P-SB11. We could see and talk to a spirit and the EMF meters would be steady green. As Tonya always says, "Your own bodies are the best equipment there is." Hair standing up on your arms, or a feeling of nausea or an energy surge in your gut is often your best indicator (which goes back to developing and trusting your intuition). Besides, the spirits can manipulate cameras, the P-SB11, and any electronic device. They are famous for it. As much as we love to get total corroboration of data—seeing a spirit, communicating with it through the P-SB11, getting a temperature change, and having the EMF meter spike—it is rare for all these things to happen at once. Technology is just one tool. Using all of the tools in this chapter in conjunction is a more comprehensive approach that will yield better results.

Don't Change the Question to Accommodate the Answer
Test What You Can

We are all looking for physical evidence. Almost without exception, our guests at the Webb thought this meant photographic evidence. This was often the hardest to verify, however, because of the way light and shadow play (especially through windows) and the human predisposition toward *pareidolia*, which is the mind's need to make order of the unfamiliar. It often tends to do this by tricking us into thinking we are seeing faces where there are none.

We were careful to try to reproduce the lighting, angles, and conditions whenever we thought we had a photo of a spirit at the Webb. We do the same when one is sent to us by a colleague or a guest after an investigation. It is always hard to disappoint someone who thinks they caught the image of a spirit in cases where it is *pareidolia*. Early on in our Webb investigation we received a photo from a guest investigator that excited our interest. We jumped in the car on a Sunday afternoon and made the trip to the Webb, only to find it was an oddly shaped planter and its fake flowers and *not* the gargoyle-faced demon we thought we were all seeing.

We also have a trusted team of fellow researchers who analyze our photos without any background data.

In the case of slamming doors, lights coming on, objects moving, and similar phenomena we did our best to look at all the mundane possibilities and tried to replicate as many of the contributing elements as we could. Only then would we consider it as paranormal. In most instances, it was firmly in the realm of CAP: *conditional* anomalous phenomena. That is the hard fact of this kind of work. We never can be sure.

Corroborate What You Can

Our trusted team of researchers can be invaluable for photo analysis, but they all live many hours away, so we looked to historians, fellow researchers, and sensitives and mediums who joined us on the investigation to corroborate what we were experiencing. Being able to go into the Webb more than 70 times over two years allowed us to track and catalog character and story "arcs" as they changed.

Joey's position as creative director with the local historical education tour company during the investigations also proved invaluable, as he spent over two years researching local lore. The revenge story of the two sisters we shared in Chapter 2—where one is the jealous spinster and the other the beautiful one who gets engaged—happens to be prevalent in the area and is attached to a home in Beaufort as well. Joey found other prevalent themes of local hauntings that had also attached themselves to the Webb.

We find that the more people we talk to, the more we can distinguish between paranormal phenomena attached to a building or geographical area and myth and lore.

Know the Difference Between Skepticism, Over-Enthusiasm, and Cynicism

Ideally, even the most seasoned investigator should have some *skepticism*—this is what allows us to be rigorous in our research, testing, and corroboration. There is so much we still don't know.

We often asked ourselves why people came to the Webb investigations. It was surprising how high a percentage of people could not articulate it when asked. By and large, those who were able to answer were either looking for proof of life after death or had experienced things and were hungry to make sense of them. Tonya helped many people process their prior experiences through our common experiences at the Webb.

We had about five percent of visitors that we termed *over-enthusiastic*. Every creak was a ghost; every shadow on a photo was a ghost; they constantly felt like they were being watched, prodded, or followed. To them, it was *all* anomalous phenomena. This could make for a long and frustrating night. Sometimes the over-enthusiastic, in their zeal for an experience, inadvertently disrespected the spirits. A haunted venue is not a zoo or a museum where the spirits are on display. As you've seen from the interactions detailed in this book, if we barraged a spirit with questions, they either stopped responding or responded with sarcasm or understandable anger.

It was rare, but there were times when we had *cynics* join the investigation. Unlike *skeptics*, who were open to the possibilities, cynics had their minds made up that the Webb was either a funhouse where everything was rigged to fool them, that we were lying, or that we were playing some type of psychological mind game. To them, *nothing* was anomalous phenomena. *Cynicism* contributed little to the investigation and their relentless debunking made things difficult. The "resident cynic" is another trend from the "reality" shows that paranormal investigators need to be aware of.

Closing Thoughts

The spirits of the Webb—both transient and those that have been there for a long time and may be for a long time to come—were certainly at times tricksters who had more than their share of fun with us. They also taught us a great deal about compassion, boundaries, the nature of life and death, and our prejudices and fears. For that, we will always be grateful.

By way of an ending, we leave you with this: One night in the fall of 2016 a reservation for 13 appeared in the booking system. We waited for the text or phone call from the booking agent to let us know that an investigation was on for the night. As the time for us to leave for the Webb approached, we still hadn't gotten any word. Mysteriously, the booking had disappeared. No credit card transactions, calls, or evidence of who the 13 were or how this happened was ever found. Keep in mind, a reservation cannot be made in the system without a credit card, name, and phone number. Although the reservation was witnessed by several staff members, Joey and Tonya included, no record remained of the reservation the following day.

Was it the Webb, which we hadn't visited in several weeks, calling us back?

Given all that we've reported in this book, how can we say no?

BIBLIOGRAPHY

Abram, David. *The Spell of the Sensuous* (New York: Vintage Books, 1996), 89.

Goldhamer, Rabbi Douglas with Peggy Bagley. *Healing through God's Love: Kabbalah's Hidden Secrets* (Burdett, NY: Larson Publications, 2015), 38.

Hawking, Stephen. *A Brief History of Time: From the Big Bang to Black Holes* (New York: Bantam, 1988), ix.

Horden, William Douglas. *Way of the Diviner* (CreateSpace, 2016), 121.

Suzuki, Shunryu. *Zen Mind, Beginner's Mind* (Boston, MA: Shambhala, 2011), 16.

ABOUT THE AUTHORS

Tonya Madia, RYT, RMT, LMT is an author, Reiki Master, medium, yoga teacher, and massage therapist who believes in the importance of cultivating and trusting your intuition. She has seen firsthand how practices such as yoga, meditation, and Reiki lead to a deeper awareness and understanding of the natural intuitive abilities that we all possess and she now teaches others how to develop these life-enhancing skills. Her lifelong experiences with the paranormal and encounters as a medium have led her to state with surety that consciousness does survive the death of the physical body. She has been invited to investigate everything from private residences and cemeteries to retail stores and community centers and feels extremely blessed to be called on so often to help others on their life journey. She is the author of *Living the Intuitive Life: Cultivating Extraordinary Awareness* (Visionary Living, 2017) and offers workshops on developing intuition, yoga, meditation, and dreamwork as well as private readings. Her website is tonyamadia.com

Joey Madia, when he is not investigating strange phenomena, is an award-winning screenwriter, audio dramatist, playwright, novelist, actor, and director. His screenplay *The Man at the Foot of the Bed* (based on a true story by Josette Saginario) has been a two-time Official Selection and a Beverly Hills Film Festival invitee. He is the author of four books on using theater in the classroom (The *Stage Learning Series*, Accompany Publishing, 2007) and is working on a fifth book, *Every Day is a Story All its Own*, about the art, craft, and importance of telling our stories.

189

His award-winning poetry, nonfiction essays, and short stories have been widely published. He is the author of two novels: *Jester-Knight* (New Mystics, 2009) and *Minor Confessions of an Angel Falling Upward* (Burning Bulb Publishing, 2012). His website is joeymadia.com. He also has profiles at OnStellar, Stage 32, Goodreads, Film Freeway, and IMDb.

Outside the Webb the night of our thirtieth investigation.

CPSIA information can be obtained
at www.ICGtesting.com
Printed in the USA
BVHW032043031218
534671BV00001B/50/P